HYBRIDS

SO YOU THINK
YOU ARE HUMAN

TANIS HELLIWELL

Library and Archives Canada Cataloguing in Publication

Helliwell, Tanis, author

Hybrids : so you think you are human / by Tanis Helliwell.

Includes bibliographical references and index.

ISBN 978-1-987831-01-6

     1. Leprechauns. 2. Spirits. 3. Elves. 4. Angels.
5. Giants. 6. Spirituality. 7. New Age movement. I. Title.

BF1552.H44 2015   133.1'4   C2015-902033-6

Cover by Nita Alvarez and Melany Hallam

Published by Wayshower Enterprises

www.iitransform.com

NOTE TO THE READER

This book was co-created by Tanis Helliwell and Lloyd the Leprechaun, also known as The Grand. Tanis had the not-so-exciting task of providing the facts about each hybrid described herein, whereas I, Lloyd, added me personal understanding of these magnificent beings. To further enhance, many individuals who believe they are from these various hybrid evolutions tell their wonderful stories (anonymously, of course). We hope you enjoy our book as much as we have enjoyed writing it.

CONTENTS

CONTENTS

INTRODUCTION

by Tanis Helliwell

This is a controversial book. It will be confusing to some, offensive to a few, and confirming for others.

I have been teaching workshops on the topic of human hybrids for some years, and many people attending the workshops felt that, at long last, the reasons for their feelings of being different in a human world were answered.

When I first became a psychotherapist in my twenties, I did so—I thought at the time—to help humans. During my thirties and forties, although I continued working with humans, it became increasingly obvious to me that not all humans were as they appeared on the surface. They were different in ways that could not be explained by traditional psychotherapeutic approaches. This discovery took me on a journey that has evolved over the years into the topic of this book: *Hybrids: So You Think You Are Human.*

My first breakthrough into this new world of learning occurred when I rented a cottage in Ireland that was occupied by a Leprechaun family. The fact that the cottage was haunted by the little people was well known to the village locals, but was a great surprise to me as I had rented the cottage sight unseen.

The head of the Leprechaun family, who uses the pseudonym of Lloyd, taught me a great deal about Elementals—nature spirits and little people by other names—and asked me to write a book about

Elementals in ten years. This I did in *Summer with the Leprechauns*, and later in a second book titled *Pilgrimage with the Leprechauns*.

During that intervening decade, between living in the cottage and writing the first book, people with Elemental ancestry came to my therapy practice, and it was recognizing their ancestry that enabled me to help them fulfill their purpose in this life.

I came to think of them as "hybrids". As you can imagine, it was a bit of a stretch to find myself in this foreign land with no guideposts, other than intuition, on how to assist them.

I was getting quite good at recognizing and assisting Elemental hybrids when, lo and behold, other people came to me who did not have Elemental ancestry—but who were not fully human.

There are other types of hybrids?

This was a greater stretch. What helped me was knowing that my acceptance of Elemental hybrids was helping people. You might ask how these individuals even found me. It's not that I had a calling card that read:

> *"Specializing in Hybrid Psychotherapy: Come to me to discover why you feel different from other humans."*

It has surprised me that hybrids have become such a major theme in my life, because I thought for many years that my work in the world, as a psychotherapist and teacher in both mainstream and spiritual workshops, was to help humans to develop their consciousness. Looking back, I realize that cosmic intelligence wanted information about hybrids to be accessible to all beings that live on Earth, and that Spirit needed a mouthpiece for this information.

I got the job. For the past twenty years, I have taught both elemental and hybrid workshops around the world. After hearing my talks, people urged me to write this book.

Although there is currently a vast amount of information

available on Angels and Elementals, I feel the time is ripe for introducing the possibility that not all humans are fully human. I say "possibility" because I want you to decide the truth of this for yourself. I also want to make it clear that my references to hybrids do not refer to UFO abductees who think they have been impregnated by alien beings. Although this topic bears investigation, it is not the topic of this book.

The hybrids to which I am referring have been on our planet for eons of time and are approved by the great spiritual beings who oversee the destiny of this planet.

HYBRIDS: So You Think You Are Human provides information on the most common hybrids I have discovered to date, with personal stories from people who believe themselves to be hybrids. This list continues to grow as I discover more types of hybrids.

I also include a short questionnaire—*What Type of Hybrid Am I?*—to help you determine if perhaps you are a hybrid, along with helpful hints to assist you if you find that you are.

Hybrids have been here all along, but I was not ready to consider this at an earlier time. The immensity of the material would have overwhelmed me and I might have rejected it. Spirit leads us step by step when it brings us into unknown territory so that we can succeed in absorbing the learning it wishes to give us when the time is right for us to receive it. Life offers us opportunities to give up our preconceptions about what is—and what is not—possible. The more open we are to what the universe wants to present, the more we are able to see clearly what has been in front of our eyes all the time. Hybrids is one of those themes for me.

It is my hope that you will find it to be an interesting concept as well, and, if Spirit wills, it may offer insight to unanswered questions in your life about who you are and why you do what you do.

Am I a Hybrid?

The following thoughts are common to hybrids. If you answer "yes" to many of these statements, this book will be of special interest to you.

- I often feel I don't fit in
- I am hypersensitive to violence
- I am deeply committed to helping the Earth
- I would describe myself as an independent thinker
- I follow my own inner guidance about rightness, even if it goes against the norm

INTRODUCTION

by Lloyd the Leprechaun

*L*loyd here! For those of you who don't know me, I've been
working with Tanis for a couple of decades now and we've
co-written a few books together. I am a Leprechaun and my father
and mother were Leprechaun, descended from a long line of
Leprechauns. In my world, the realm of the Elementals—Nature
Spirits by another name—I'm given over to the study of humans,
especially how humans and Elementals can work together as co-
creators on this planet. This is what we're supposed to be doing ...
if you hadn't realized it.

For most of me adult life, I've been working with various kinds of
Elementals, Goblins, Gnomes, Elves and such—you get the picture—
to make sure they're up to the task of collaborating with humans
who want to partner and create a beautiful planet in alignment with
natural and spiritual laws. At least that's how my work started.
However, it's taken a few jogs in the road and that brings us to the
topic at hand: Elementals who have entered the human world as
what we're calling "hybrids".

You might wonder why Elementals would want to do such
a thing?

We wouldn't—if humans took better care of OUR
environment—but they don't. As the areas on Earth where we can
live are shrinking, many of us thought that, as humans, we could

develop our free will to become full creators to help the Earth by saving the environment, as well as bringing more beauty and joy into the human world. After all, we have always been way ahead of humans in the creative arts—painting, dance, theatre, etc.

That's not to say that Elementals are able to bring one hundred percent of themselves into the human world. Even our old ones were only able to retain about twenty to twenty-five percent of their Elemental heritage. That's because humans have such strong egos that Elementals wouldn't be able to cope and could easily lose themselves in humanity. As such, only the strongest—usually the eldest—received permission by the Karmic Boards of the Elementals and Humans to enter human evolution.

That's the way it is with hybrids generally speaking. Angel hybrids, for example, are only a small percent Angel with the greatest percentage remaining human.

All this hybrid incarnating has been going on for a few thousand years, but more so in the last five hundred years until Elementals found the way to stay in our own world while working with humans—which is the work me and Tanis are doing now.

I'd like to point out, and this is important, that even as I remain in my Elemental world, working with a human has changed me ... and it's changed Tanis as well. That's because we become who we associate with. It's the power of thought that makes us who and what we are.

And that's exactly how hybrids are determined by the Karmic Boards. The Great Ones who oversee our evolution can hear, see, and know what Spirit wants, and they then think what Spirit wants into form.

Elementals do this and humans do this; but unless the humans are spiritual masters, they don't have the rightness of it the way Elementals do. You humans never have been good listeners of the Divine Plan. Instead you have thought up a world with polluted water and air, violence and what-not, but I'd better not go down that track. You humans are not too good at facing yourselves in the mirror!

So now I'll turn this back to me favorite writing partner, Tanis, who will guide you through all the scientific, historical, and mythical information about hybrids (according to humans, that is). Then I'll step back in to provide my up-close perspective and fill in anything she may have missed.

Stay posted ... it's going to get very exciting!

THE CASE FOR HYBRIDS

It is an accepted fact that humans and all life on Earth evolved over millennia from chemical compounds on a gaseous planet. Although we accept this fact intellectually, most of us have no emotional connection to it. It is not part of our experiential reality and, because of this, our life is based on an altogether different belief system. That is: All humans are basically the same and the only ways we differ are in race, culture, gender, skin and hair color, height, and weight.

This view of a human being prevails, even though science has proven that all humans are ninety-nine percent ether—not the physical matter we erroneously see ourselves as.

If we cannot see the basic facts of reality, how can we hope to perceive the complexity and variations of being human?

The good news is that most scientists now accept a relatively new principle: Thoughts can change the result of their experiments and might even deny the validity of the results, if the results do not tally with their belief systems.

Example: In 1992, in Naturwissenschaften 79:358 German scientist Svetla Balabanova and two colleagues reported findings of cocaine, hashish, and nicotine in Egyptian mummies dating from 1070 BCE to 395 AD. They were denounced by many of their colleagues who said that it was impossible, and that someone must have put it there because tobacco came from the New World and was only discovered by Columbus in the early sixteenth century. Recent investigation has re-established the credibility of their findings.

We also now know there has been communication between North America, Europe, and Asia for thousands of years. An early stone-age tool called the Clovis Point, used by the ancestors of the Lascaux caves about thirty thousand years ago, has recently been found in North America. The Ojibwa people, who live around the Great Lakes in North America, have an unusual mitochondrial DNA found in Europe over fifteen thousand years ago.

It takes courage to go against prevailing opinion but, like the German scientist, we must or we will never learn the truth about our existence on Earth.

I learned this early in life. In my first book, *Decoding Destiny*, published in 1988, I stated that Atlanteans built the Sphinx around 10,000 BCE. At that time, it was accepted by archeologists that the Sphinx was less than half that age, and it was emotionally difficult for me to assert something that contradicted "experts". Since then, American geologist Robert Schoch did a computer analysis showing that the Sphinx is between ten thousand and fifteen thousand years old—and eroded by water—which tallies with my premise that it was damaged with the sinking of Atlantis.

We're at a wonderful time on Earth—when our preconceptions of our entire history are being re-examined. We have been taught to believe that all humans evolved from the apes and, even though archeologists have not yet found the "missing link", they are convinced a skull will be discovered to prove their theory. Funnily, the more skulls archeologists discover, the more they change their earlier opinions—but they cling to each opinion as solid and correct at the time.

Biologists aren't having an easy time understanding what a human is either. They have only been able to decode the purpose of three to five percent of our DNA; the remainder of the DNA they term "junk DNA", which means "ignore it—it's not important".

When they learn more, I believe 1) they will discover we're not all one hundred percent human, or 2) change their view of what human is. Do we see anywhere in nature where this has happened? The answer is "Of course!"

The most obvious observation is that all beings on the Earth— including plants, animals, humans, stones, fish, birds, totally distinct species of beings of absolutely all life—evolved from the same chemical stew billions of years ago. Isn't it amazing that this happened, but humanity didn't do it? This evolution happened before we could even dream of creating such forms of life. Obviously, there is a Plan that continues to unfold without us.

Nature working with this Divine Plan continues to evolve many types of hybrids—not just one animal, one plant, one kind of human being. And this is happening today—not just in the past.

Where I live in Canada, we have two kinds of bears who have created a hybrid offspring. As the northern ice started to melt due to global warming, the polar bear's habitat decreased and their numbers began to decline rapidly, with the increasing possibility of their extinction. Simultaneously, because of the decrease in ice, the grizzly bear moved further north into the territory of the polar bear. The two species mated and have produced fertile offspring. Could this be nature ensuring that the best of the polar bear gets transferred to the new environment it will need to survive?

Here is another example of how nature has created a fertile hybrid. Many species of dolphins are known to interbreed in the wild and produce fertile offspring. Risso's Dolphin and the Bottlenose Dolphin have done this, but the best known is a fertile hybrid from a False Killer Whale and Bottlenose Dolphin—called the Wolphin.

In human history, we know now that Neanderthal and Cro-Magnon man mated and created fertile hybrids. If Spirit is continually working through nature creating hybrid animals, as it appears to be doing, could Spirit also be working through humanity to develop many different hybrids? I believe the answer is a resounding "Yes".

I'd like to add one more thought when considering the possibility of various hybrids. Well-respected researchers think that artificial intelligence is developing so fast that humans and machines (artificial intelligence) will merge within the next forty to fifty years. People favoring this premise call themselves "transhumanists" and the result is called a human-machine-hybrid.

Cyborgs, as they are known in some science fiction books and movies, are moving ever closer to more sophisticated realization. For instance, inventions that link brain cells by means of microchips have already been made. These coming developments show how serious the hybrid issue is.

This book does not deal with the topic of human-machine-hybrids. However, I believe that in our near future we will have to deal with this essential question: What is human? Dealing with this question now in the context of intelligent hybrids who exist within the human race will help us approach the topic of human-machine hybrids in the future. Hopefully it will also allow hybrids who are already here to accept their uniqueness with more ease.

Accepting these possibilities will set us on a path to deeper understanding of our differences and the gifts each of us can offer to the world. It turns our world from black and white to a multitude of rich colors as we discover our talents, weaknesses, reasons for living, and how to co-create together on this wonderful planet.

So let's journey beyond the superficiality of skin and hair color and delve more deeply into our inner being to see what we can learn. Let's talk to individuals who believe they are a hybrid and hear what they have to say. Perhaps you, too, will discover that you are a hybrid.

Let the journey begin.

HOW HYBRIDS ARE CREATED

We humans have been creating hybrids for a long time. We crossed a peach and a plum and the result was a delicious nectarine, which is fertile and can produce fruit for many years. However, not all of our creations are in keeping with Divine Law.

Some hybrids are not positive in the long term; this is especially evident today concerning seeds. Monsanto and DuPont created sterile hybrid seeds to sell to farmers. Sterile seeds may result in higher yields for a year, but farmers, especially in poor countries, cannot afford to buy more sterile seeds every year. Ancient seeds are well adapted to the environment in which they are grown, and if they are lost to our common seed bank, we will become more susceptible to plague and worldwide famine

Some hybrid plants apparently cause disease in humans. This is probable with the wheat we consume in the western world. Celiac disease, diabetes, arthritis, heart disease, and a host of other maladies appear related to wheat, which has undergone several profit-driven modifications over the last few hundred years.

Humans have also created hybrid animals, such as the mule, a sterile cross between a horse and donkey, to have the benefits of both parent animals. Some of these animal crosses are positive and in accordance with Divine Law, whereas some are not. The pig was created in Atlantis by crossing an animal with a primitive human. Jews, Muslims, and Hindus might have forgotten the reason for their taboo against eating pork, but it was considered to be a kind of cannibalism. Pork sits in the digestive track and rots quickly. The human body cannot differentiate between itself and the pork, so it does not digest properly.

Pigskin is used in skin grafts for humans and pig heart valves are used in human heart operations. People in survival situations who have had to eat human flesh state that it tastes like pork, and some primitive cannibalistic cultures have referred to human flesh as "long pig".

We are able to physically create hybrids and the more we learn about various genes, the more technically skilled we become. Are humans equally skilled at knowing how to create hybrids according to the spiritual laws of the Divine Plan? A person would need to be an enlightened being to know these spiritual laws and have the wisdom to apply them. How many of us qualify?

The good news is that humans, as a race, are rising in consciousness and are beginning to value the qualities that lead to enlightenment. As we purify our thoughts and emotions to acquire, as the Buddhists say, "right motivation for our actions", we raise our frequency and realize when our actions are not in accordance with Spirit. It then becomes offensive to us to engage in these actions.

We are evolving from animal man to true human. Animal man is concerned only with the physical and how to conquer nature, whereas enlightened man is motivated to co-create with nature according to spiritual laws. As we evolve into enlightened beings, it is my premise that we will discover that, not only plants and animals on this planet are hybrids, but there are human hybrids as well.

Human folklore, myths, and religions around the world discuss the existence of intelligent non-human beings who are interacting with humans. This could be Angels, Birds, Giants, and Dragons and each of these types is found in many unrelated cultures. These beings are often referred to as gods with special and unique powers that humans do not have. In our myths, such as those of the Olympian gods of Greece, these beings bred with humans to create fertile hybrids, who have semi-divine powers and strengths. Even in contemporary religions like Christianity, the Virgin Mary is believed to have been impregnated by the Holy Spirit to create Jesus the Christ, a semi-divine being.

Spirit is continually creating hybrids in our natural world, as demonstrated by the previously mentioned examples. Great beings, existing in higher dimensions than our physical reality, work with spiritual laws to create the diversity of hybrids existing on our planet. They do this through the power of thought. As shown by quantum physics, we know our thoughts create our reality. If we humans, in our virtual infancy in the Universe, can understand this theory and learn how to practice it—by healing ourselves and others through prayer and by manifesting what we desire—then just imagine the tremendous creative power of the great beings overseeing our evolution? What we think of as miracles today will be talents we all possess when we become enlightened.

The creation of a human hybrid requires two things working simultaneously: our physical and spiritual ancestry. Each of us has a "body elemental" that builds our physical, emotional, and mental bodies at the time of conception when the egg and the sperm meet. Working under the guidance of the Karmic Board (great spiritual beings who oversee our evolution), it incorporates the exact parts of our individual ancestries into our unique body vessel that gives us the ability to accomplish our soul's purpose in this life.

The same body elemental that builds the body in this lifetime has built the body in all lifetimes. It knows all of our past, our present history, and even our future potential. The body elemental knows our physical ancestry as it relates to genes inherited from our parents and ancestors. It also knows our spiritual ancestry: who we were in past lives, as well as the countries and races wherein we have roots.

Our spiritual and physical ancestry are mixed in our blood.

Our real essence—who we really are, not just genetically, but spiritually—is found in our blood. Scientists have not yet discovered this because their measurements do not take into account the etheric essence of the blood. Although they may have forgotten the real reason, this is the spiritual reason behind religions that ban blood transfusions. It is well-documented that individuals who received a heart transplant often develop new interests and dietary cravings that were characteristic of their heart donor. For example, a vegetarian cannot wait to eat a hamburger after the procedure. Investigation reveals that the heart came from a young man who loved hamburgers.

To enter human evolution as a hybrid, all beings must request permission from both the Karmic Board of Humans and that of his or her origin. There are different requirements of individuals from each of these ancestors of today's hybrids.

When an Elemental, for example, applies to enter human evolution, the Karmic Board makes certain the being is strong enough to withstand the human will. In the Elemental's first human life, the hybrid might only be allowed ten percent of his/her ancestry, whereas by the tenth lifetime, the individual might be strong enough to bring in twenty percent of the ancestry. So the longer a hybrid has been in human evolution, the more that individual realizes his/her own uniqueness. At the same time, he/she is better able to function in the human world, and having learned human laws, often wishes to investigate his/her original heritage.

One of the primary reasons for this book is to assist these individuals.

Within one family, there may be several kinds of hybrids. The mother might be an Angel hybrid, while the father is an Elf hybrid. They breed and create a fertile offspring, who might spiritually inherit either or both of the parents' origins, or be entirely different.

Siblings could be different types of hybrids as well.

An individual may have received permission to enter human evolution through these specific parents because they all have a karmic connection that can resolve itself better if they are members of the same family. So as not to be confusing, each of the twenty-two hybrid species will be dealt with as unique later in the book.

You might be wondering if you could be more than one hybrid and the answer is a "conditional yes". It depends on the category of hybrid. If you are originally from another star system (see Section Three), it is possible that you have entered more than one race on Earth to experience and help each of those races.

For example: The Pleiadians have been involved in the evolutions of the Green Race, Dolphins, and Whales. Therefore, it is possible to be originally from the Pleiades and feel this star is your origin— while feeling simultaneously that you are a Merperson, Dolphin, or Whale hybrid. Or if your parents are from two different hybrid evolutions, you might indentify with both of their hybrid types because you inherited the physical genes of both parents.

People often ask, "Can we return to our original origins after we have become hybrids?" It is only on our present level of consciousness that this question is important. Because everything about each of us is recorded in the Akashic Records (also known as the Book of Life), no information is ever lost. It includes our original origin and the many lives we have had in other evolutions.

In higher dimensions, we are all unique and the same simultaneously, and the question of returning to what one was in the past is of no importance. Even though we are hybrids, we may not have a conscious memory of this, but when we learn about the various types of hybrids, the information rings true and makes great sense to us.

WHAT TYPE OF HYBRID AM I?

There are many kinds of hybrids evolving on Earth. We will examine three major categories in this book. As the investigation of hybrids is still in its infancy, many types of hybrids are emerging and may be addressed at a later time.

The three major categories of Hybrids:

1. **Elementals** – include Leprechauns, Brownies, Pixies, Goblins, Trolls, Forest Elves, Royal Elves, and Tree Devas. These are the original inhabitants of the Earth who have entered human evolution.
2. **Human Cousins** – include Inner Earthlings, Merpersons, Dolphins, and Whales, all descendents from early humans.
3. **Star Beings** – include Angels, Els, Horuses, Pans, Dragons, Bees, Anunnakis, Centaurs, and possibly others who entered human evolution as hybrids.

Types of Hybrids

What follows is detailed analysis about the twenty-two different types of hybrids I have discovered and worked with closely. You may immediately recognize the specific type of hybrid you are—Elemental, Human Cousin, Star Being—or you may relate to several different types as you read the various descriptions and Helpful Hints at the end of each hybrid segment.

After you've read the book, the "What Type of Hybrid Am I?" questionnaire on page 171 will further assist you in recognizing which of type of hybrid you might be, or in which you have had other incarnations.

Relax and enjoy investigating this possible new aspect of your humanity. Allow your natural instincts to guide you as you follow your heart.

SECTION I:

ELEMENTAL HYBRIDS

*L*loyd here again and, as promised, I'm going to talk about
  the various kinds of Elemental hybrids. We call ourselves
"Elemental" because we are made up of the elements of earth,
air, fire, and water. As a Leprechaun, I'm an earth Elemental.
More of us incarnate in human evolution than the other kinds. Still,
I'd like to give you an idea about the others in case you are one of
them, as it sometimes happens.

Air, water, and fire Elementals often choose to partner with a
human while remaining in the Elemental world rather than entering
human evolution as a hybrid. Their nature is so very different from
humans that it would be difficult for them to live as a human.

Air Elementals are called Sylphs and they look after the weather
patterns; water Elementals are called Undines and they are found
in tiny creeks all the way up to gigantic waterfalls, like your mighty
Niagaras. The last are Salamanders and they work with fire—right
from the kundalini energy within your bodies to the ones who bring
the energy of the Sun to the Earth.

Earth Elementals—those most likely to enter your world as
hybrids—have a hereditary, graduated clan system. These clans are
divided into kings, princes, nobles, and a variety of craft guilds.
The craft guilds specialize in color, sound, aroma, and working
with the elements (air/ fire/water/earth). Included in these clans are
hunters, musicians, legend weavers, clothiers, storytellers, artists,
magicians, healers, and warriors, to name a few. Each clan has a
specific purpose to accomplish that which is instinctive to its nature.
Elementals, unlike humans, do not think in terms of wanting

to change jobs and, when Elementals enter human evolution as hybrids, they often gravitate to occupations that align to their clan because it is the easiest thing to do.

LEPRECHAUN

*I*t's time to start talking about earth Elementals and, as you can imagine, I'd like to start with Leprechauns. Folks are always wondering if Leprechauns are found only in Ireland and the answer is "No"; we've got cousins in other parts of the world.

In the Netherlands, they are called Kabouters and, like us, they tend to have beards and are good craftspeople. In former times, they often lived underground in forests and, let's not forget they like mushrooms … God's food.

Leprechauns are known to have a bit of the trickster in them, but I'd say that's unfair. We're just smart. Some of us craftspeople are making shoes and clothes and the like, but you could say that was in the olden days and not so common now. However, 'tis true that we do like doing crafts, pottery, wood carving, sculpture, all these kinds of things and, when we enter human evolution as hybrids, you can sometimes find us making craft … and being crafty (smile)!

There are other professions in which Leprechauns excel. We are great bankers and keep the accounts for a lot of Royal Elves, who are better at spending than earning money. We're known for keeping money close to us and for striking a good bargain … we know a good deal when we see it.

I think of myself as a philosopher and a scholar and some

Leprechaun hybrids take that route in the human world. Still, I wouldn't say it is our major talent. We are as diverse as individuals as you humans are, but I'm attempting here to find common things that you humans might notice.

Well, I guess body shape is one thing. You might call Leprechaun hybrids stocky or portly ... not as svelte as Elves. And we often have a bit of body hair and some of us keep beards and are proud of them.

Come to think of it, I think our best virtue is our humor. Sometimes humans like to comment on our wit and good sense of humor. Comedians Robin Williams, Jonathan Winters, and W. C. Fields all had many qualities you could attribute to Leprechaun hybrids, if you were going to point fingers, which of course, I'm not. We'll never be the leading man in the movies, but we'll win you over with our personality. Occasionally humans might find us "touchy", especially if they're poking fun at us, but let's just say we've got our pride.

The greatest lesson for us Leprechauns to learn is not to take advantage of others and to be able to laugh at ourselves as easily as we laugh at others. We can learn to do this by working co-operatively in partnerships instead of alone, which is our natural inclination because we are so very independent.

Tanis is giving me a nudge that I should mention relationship issues, but that's a bit sensitive for us. We're closed-mouthed when it comes to our private business and that includes relationships with our mates. You could look at that as a characteristic of Leprechaun hybrids. We're not much for flaunting our sexuality, as Elves do. To be truthful, though I may regret saying it, we have a bit of self-consciousness and insecurity about not being as beautiful as some others ... like the leading man.

And now, a little note from my co-writer Tanis.

Many individuals, who will remain anonymous in this book, think of themselves as hybrids and Lloyd and I are grateful to them for relating their stories to help others better understand the various types of hybrids.

✎ Leprechaun Hybrid: SALLY

Sally said that she was a Leprechaun who developed Troll qualities early in life to protect herself in an unwelcoming and even hostile environment. Sally is short and stocky; private about any sexual questions.

> "I usually see humor in most situations … even those others would find no humor in at all. Mentally, I am a bit of a philosopher—love learning new things to the point of boring others to tears with my knowledge—and yet unable to stop because I find it all so very interesting. I don't take much stock in acting spiritual anymore, but love to be close to nature, and have a sixth sense about people, animals, and other things.
>
> "I am good in business, but not in an overt way, and tend to work better behind the scenes. I love to negotiate the type of transaction where all parties benefit. Some of the negotiations I made at a very young age later enabled me to succeed financially, despite circumstances that would have left others destitute. I knew the other parties had benefitted at the time, but one family later told me exactly how serious their circumstances had been when I helped them.
>
> "The reason I do not like to be in the forefront in business is that I have a low tolerance for 'BS'. I become

protective of those who are treated unfairly, and defensive against people who do not deal fairly with others. People who wish to cheat others often keep their distance from me. It makes it difficult for me to be involved in negotiations I am not comfortable with, or in business dealings that involve coping with too many people at one time. It amazes me how many times in my life I have been one of the only ones to realize that someone was trying to cheat others. People become angry with me for not getting on board with what is happening—until they realize I am right, sometimes many years down the road. In the meantime, I often find my position to be extremely uncomfortable.

"The Leprechaun in me takes a huge amount of enjoyment in being involved in a good prank. But it is very important there's no harm done and that everyone can look back and have a good chuckle. But even well-meaning pranks, if done in excess, become tiresome to me.

"Another aspect of my nature is that I am doggedly determined and do not stop trying when most other people would just give up. I am a person who, when I get knocked down, keeps getting up again. The positive side to this is I have managed to overcome occurrences that would have destroyed many a person. The negative side is that sometimes I'll keep at something I should have given up … which can sometimes make me grouchy.

"My uncle was very much a Leprechaun. In his final years, he'd open up the door, stark naked, to greet the nurse who came every morning. He said he didn't want to keep them waiting and figured a nurse should be accustomed to such things. When I told him that the nurses wouldn't mind waiting for him to dress before opening the door, he'd grin a very leprechaun-ish grin.

"I was surprised to learn that, without being overt about it, he had gone to great lengths to protect and look after me and knew that I, more than anyone else he knew, would go to great lengths to do the same for him."

BROWNIE

E *nough on Leprechauns: Let's have a look at Brownies now ... the same ones folks call Tomte in Scandinavia, Domovoi in Russia, and Heinzelmannchen in Germany. Brownies and Pixies (that's what Gnomes call themselves in various parts of England) are distant cousins to Leprechauns. But we're all Gnomes.*

Brownies like to live right alongside humans, such as in their houses and on their farms. In the olden days, even up to the mid-eighteenth century, humans would leave a little milk and honey out, sometimes even porridge, for Elemental helpers as a thank-you, but this disappeared with the disappearance in their belief in us.

The chief characteristic of Brownies and Brownie hybrids is they want to be helpful and well-liked.

Tanis has two friends, a man and a woman, who are Brownie hybrids. And when she has a dinner party and the rest of the folks are still sitting at the table, the Brownie hybrids are up doing the dishes. This is typical of Brownie hybrids, especially in the areas of home and garden.

Often a Brownie hybrid will marry an Angel or a Dragon hybrid, because they want to look after somebody. We know a Brownie hybrid who married an Angel. The husband is busy thinking noble thoughts for the good of humanity and she is looking after the home and garden. She grounds him so that he is better able to do his work in the world.

Brownies have difficulty saying "No" and don't like to complain. As such, they can build up resentments. They will suddenly blow up or leave a situation that is oppressing them. This is especially true if they feel their needs are not being recognized or appreciated— or both.

The greatest learning for Brownies is moderation. They are natural helpers; yet they need to learn boundaries so that others do not take advantage of their good nature. They also need to learn the amount to do which is healthy for them ... not to overwork. They are so good at what they do to make things cozy for others that they will just keep on doing until they are exhausted.

✦ Brownie Hybrid: LUCY

"I have difficulties in making choices. Often I will choose caring or looking after another person, sometimes to the detriment of my own well-being. Then I feel drained and in need of time and space to recover my energy. One difficulty my family has experienced is my reluctance to speak out about things that bother me for fear I will hurt another's feelings. This can result in discomfort to myself.

"My gifts are that I enjoy the company of others very much, either one-on-one or in groups. I often take on the role of organizer and delegator for group get-togethers, both work and pleasure. I am also a collaborator, enjoying group efforts toward a shared goal. I will be the one in the group who takes on the role of mediator when

misunderstanding or conflict arises. I spend some of my
leisure time contemplating our shared existence on this
planet and how best to spend the time we've been given
here. I often encourage others to take the time to also think
about life and the ways in which we are all connected.

"One of my greatest gifts of contribution is that I share
my appreciation and gratefulness for all of life through my
words, my gestures, and my writing. The greatest lesson I
have learned is to not hold back on allowing myself to feel
sorrow and joy, pain and contentment, chaos and clarity.
All have their place; the trick is to see them as fleeting
states of mind and to allow them to flow through, and not
become fixtures within."

PIXIE

*P*ixies—the name used most in Cornwall and Devon—are
Gnomes, but different than Brownies in that they choose
to have nothing to do with humans and prefer to live in their own
communities in the countryside.

All countries have Pixies and, in Breton, they are called Korrigans.
Many Pixies apply to enter human evolution as hybrids, but few are
accepted, as they find it difficult to live alone and without their group.

In the olden days, their favorite places were those of earth power,
which is where humans often put dolmens and stone circles. Pixies,
often called Fairies by humans, were there before humans built
these structures. Let's just say that the humans and the Pixies both

knew a good thing in power spots when they saw them. In England, farmers knew to leave mushroom rings, also called Fairy rings, and rings of trees that were sacred to the Fairies. These kinds of Elementals were actually Pixies.

Pixies are usually a bit more childlike and delicate in appearance than the other gnomes we have been describing. Hobbits, in the book and film "Lord of the Rings", were modeled as a combination of Pixies and Brownies. They vary in size and can be quite small— from only a few inches tall up to half the height of a short human. More often, in the Elemental world, Pixies are one to two feet tall. One Pixie hybrid said, "I know I have wings, but I don't use them much." Having wings is typical of Pixies, and Pixie hybrids often feel they have etheric wings.

Pixies usually love music, dancing, and playing in all ways with others of their kind. They are often attracted to children and young children sometimes have Pixies as their play friends. Unlike Brownies, Pixies love the outdoors and don't like to be confined. When Pixies enter human evolution as hybrids, they dislike boundaries in any form, including physical and psychological restrictions. They are fiercely independent, yet at the same time, they yearn to be part of a group, as they were in the Elemental world. This is a big conflict —to belong or go their own way. They often move back and forth, creating conflict with their friends or lovers who don't understand what they really want.

When Pixies enter human evolution, they need to be careful not to lose themselves. They feel a great responsibility to prove they have earned the right to be a human. They need to prove this, not only for themselves, but also for the Fairy Race, which they identify as other Pixies, Brownies, and Gnomes.

➤ Pixie Hybrid: SOPHIE

"My eyes are the first thing people notice about me. They are almond-shaped and of an intensity that is rare. The color is light blue with flecks of white. My body is petite with short arms and legs. I stopped growing at age eleven and have tiny feet and hands the size of a nine-year-old girl.

"As a child, I was only happy and whole when in the woods, by a stream or lake, by myself, or with one rare dear friend. I was deeply sad in general and thought it was a mighty mistake to be on this human plane. In teen and early adult years, suicide was attempted. I trusted only animals—not humans—and gave to them my allegiance. Dolls were made out of everything from cloth to forest clay. They became my friends as I could communicate with them very effectively.

"Singing and dancing are huge for me to express sheer joy; however, I rarely let myself do it. I love foraging in the forest for winterberries, mushrooms, and adore finding Lady Slipper and Jack-in-the-Pulpit. I get Seasonal Affective Disorder (SAD) in the winter and thrive into the night in the summer. I have spent most of my life living outside my body, not even giving it its due. My greatest physical joy is being nude in water, free to move about, and exalt in life.

"My body does not tolerate human food. It would be a joy to be a breatharian who lives on air alone. Food is beautiful to look at, but I would rather photograph gorgeous fruits and vegetables than eat them. I can tell how things taste by smelling them and it is usually just as rewarding.

"Aging is a closet issue with me. Because my heart responds to wholesome beauty, the signs of irrevocable cellular failure seem unacceptable. Only by going deeper into my spiritual source, can I once again meld with all that is truly beautiful.

"Menstruation was very painful. Still, at the time of ovulation, my sexual desire was all but uncontrollable. It did seem the most beautiful and sacred communication possible. Flirtatiousness was a natural charm that became addictive behavior. Sex with humans did result in many problems. I was sexually abused from ages nine to eleven, then in my teens, and later, by a husband and a few others.

"As an adult, my marriages and childrearing were emotionally laden with strife and disappointment. I was exhausted. Only in my later years have I found any groundedness and serenity. I was completely loyal to my husbands, as I strove to be a better human. However, I would not settle for the marriages we had made, as I continuously wanted to improve them. I am now single and quite independently pleased to be chaste.

"My mind moves like lightening from one topic to another. I always asked the bigger questions and could find no answers from traditional sources. I was quick to learn and see and experience much more than others, especially in art and music. I could not figure out humans, especially their cruelty and sense of humor. Mostly, I find our mass culture to be a royal bore!

"I do not like restrictions and only want to do my work and chores when the energy is right, not when it is demanded of me. That has created friction with others when I wanted to be part of a marriage and family, but still maintain my independence.

"I enjoy being different, yet it has led to frequent bullying and harsh judgment against me, even though my differences were not harming anyone else. I am often far too naïve and give people the benefit of the doubt … until they prove unworthy of trust. I do not understand them or share my deepest private thoughts. I have had to work hard on discernment. My insights into human nature have proved too sharp for some and I have lost relationships.

"I have also had deep insecurities, believing that I am different and not in an acceptable-to-others way. I often do not understand the games people play and have to remove myself from perceived or real danger. I've spent most of my life uncomfortable as a person.

"The forest, fields, and waterfronts were my chapels; flowers were miracles. I now consider my spiritual studies to be my work and have written a performance piece that portrays the human and elfin realms warring at the expense of Mother Earth. I want to play, dance, sing, and do my heart's work. However, the laws on this planet are so heavy that I feel mired down. I want to be light and Light. There is a place in this world for difference, especially the kind that invites others to see with honor the environment in which they live.

"Hybrids sacrificed to choose a human existence in order to be helpful to Mother Nature. All humankind needs to raise consciousness and needs all support from every Light source."

GOBLIN

*L*loyd here. *Goblins and Gnomes are cousins to Brownies and Pixies. Goblins love to make fun of others and of situations. And they have a terrifically mischievous sense of humor—what in Ireland is called "black humor." If somebody falls down and breaks their leg in a funny way ... that would be very amusing to a Goblin.*

They are extremely good at holding up the mirror so you can see your real self, but not always in the nicest way. What I mean is you cannot hide from a Goblin. They can see your greatest weakness, and may regard it as their sacred duty to help you to overcome it.

In the play "King Lear", William Shakespeare got a lot of inspiration from Elementals and, by the way, many Elemental hybrids were his actors. In fact, he spent time in our Elemental world in another life. Anyway, one of the characters in King Lear is the King's Fool, who always tells the king the unwelcome truth about his daughters and others. This fool is a Goblin hybrid and, in what you humans call the Middle Ages, Goblin hybrids often found work as jesters because of their uncanny ability to mimic others perfectly. This is one of their greatest gifts.

They are the fastest of all us Elementals. They can move the fastest and get an idea the fastest. As hybrids in the human world, they make beautiful gymnasts due to their great agility and balance, and are excellent jugglers because of their hand/eye coordination.

As with Trolls, Goblins often don't have a good reputation in your children's stories, so Goblin hybrids may not trust others with their deepest selves and may armor themselves with their tongue. Goblin hybrids may be small for humans, and usually are slight of

build with slender arms and legs that may be long for their height.
Goblin hybrids might do outrageous things like stick their tongue
out at people and make comic faces and they have an athletic
elastic quality that allows their bodies and faces to contort into
many shapes—something that would horrify a Royal Elf.

Regarding relationships, Goblin hybrids might want lots of
beautiful sexual partners because they don't think they are all that
beautiful themselves They often feel unloved and misunderstood.
However, their life purpose involves them developing more loyalty,
being kinder, and committing to stay with something or with
someone, even when it is BORING. All these are qualities that
humans admire, but not something we value as highly in the
Elemental world. As such, it takes a strong will for Goblin hybrids
to practice these qualities. Still, having more will power for getting
their way than most Elementals, they can turn it towards this task.

➤ Goblin Hybrid: HANS

"As a child I was born with a crooked nose. Perhaps this is
a relic of The Fool, as in my current life I remember past
incarnations when I was a jester for a king. My mother
lovingly caressed my nose for hours to bring it into a
straight shape. If I bend my nose today, I return to feelings
of being crooked, not belonging, being at the bottom of
society. Perhaps Van Gogh cut off his ear because he also
felt crooked.

"Sexually, I am easily excited, then it quickly fades
away. It has been difficult to solve the tension between
open sexuality and loyalty to a partner. I have frequently
changed partners and had erotic attractions that I stifled
with shame, probably from being an ascetic in a monastery

in a former life.

"I have many interests, but am bored quickly. The biggest issue in my life is the tension between *wish* and *need*—on one hand, to experience a deeper bond, gratitude connection, attachment to places and persons—and on the other hand, to understand resistance, independence, being a free spirit, expressing my enthusiasm, trying new spiritual affinities, and not being bored quickly. To learn to balance these two things, I chose to be a professional gardener and worked for over twenty years in a rigid hospital setting.

"I have a bad memory and poor concentration for boring mental things; but I have a deep knowledge of what is true. I have a great desire for honesty and authenticity and want to heal the Earth. This is stronger for me than healing individuals. I have a contradictory nature: a free spirit with the need to find a teacher (but not a guru).

"The difficulties typical of my hybrid nature are: I don't deal well with material realities because they are not as important as the mind; I fear connection and commitment and often feel powerless; I recognize other hybrid Elementals as an immersion in a common field that creates in me a great longing for the lost kingdom, and a feeling that something is pulled out of my body. It is a pain like the flu.

"I have a creative, spontaneous artistic power, and can hold the mirror up to people with humor and teach them that nothing is to be taken seriously. My purpose is to establish connection to the spiritual side of Mother Nature, to serve her, and make her available to help heal people."

TROLL

*N*ext up are Trolls. Trolls are the strong men of the Elementals and they like to work with rocks. Many humans heard unflattering stories about Trolls in their childhood and are inclined not to like Trolls. Generally, Trolls and Troll hybrids either like you or they don't. They see a lot, but they don't say much. They are truly the strong, silent type. And sometimes when they do talk, it's grouchy, like complaining about someone or something. But it's not serious complaining … more the way us men like to insult the ones we like. It's the way Trolls like to communicate, and we Leprechauns get on just fine with them.

To give Tanis her due, she's very fond of Trolls because they are honest and fair. She has a woman friend, a Troll hybrid, who traveled on tours throughout the world with her. Tanis would ask her, "How is it going?" Naturally, Mary (not her real name) would grouchily complain about something or somebody. What did Tanis expect asking a Troll? It's just like dangling money in front of a Leprechaun, giving them Trolls a chance to complain. Anyway, Tanis soon saw the twinkle in Mary's eye and understood this was her way to communicate. This is often the way of a Troll.

Trolls are usually loners, but also are great protectors of those they like or admire. If you are a Troll hybrid, or have one as a friend, they will be very loyal to you—even be guardians for friends with softer natures who might be taken advantage of. Troll hybrids also guard things, as well as people and, for example, might become attracted to books or perhaps protect old buildings from demolition. Physically, Trolls are usually large, even as hybrids, and whether *they are tall, they are usually broad and have a stocky, strong build. One of the greatest learnings for Trolls and Goblins is to trust others, especially humans. Because neither of these hybrids conforms to what humans consider to be beautiful, they often have an inferiority complex, causing them to carry a chip on their shoulders. With Goblin hybrids, this can result in cutting tongues, while Trolls will often isolate themselves from folks they don't think appreciate them. Troll hybrids need to learn to forgive and let go of past injustices. This is difficult for them because they guard a sensitive heart that might have been easily hurt by someone or something.*

➤ Troll Hybrid: BETTY

"My parents were both taller than average and both my brothers are tall, but I'm short. I always knew I would not change my last name, and I have always been attracted to my own sex and did not fit into society. Books have always helped me and I have been reading since the age of three. I expect and give love, but often say things that people don't get. I feel misunderstood when I'm speaking, and sometimes people look at me like I'm crazy. I have a tendency to take things personally.

"I can read people right away and see details of their personalities. I am impatient, sometimes have a 'me first' attitude and, being self-assured, I often get what I want. I keep friends/lovers throughout my life and continue to stay in contact with them. I have 'found' important people to be in my life, even though I may lose contact with them for years.

"Nature is very important to my sense of spiritual

wholeness, and I'm interested in various aspects of all religions, but never felt comfortable with traditional church Christianity."

ELF

*T*anis thinks I might not be able to give as good an account of Elves as she can (something about being a bit hard on them), so she wants to take over now. I'll be back later.

Perhaps the largest group of Elemental hybrids that have entered human evolution are Elves. The task of many Elf hybrids is to learn to look after themselves; to be independent and fully functioning in the human world. Elf hybrids are very sensitive to their environment and cannot handle too much stress or responsibility, which can be challenging for them.

Vincent Van Gogh, for example, was likely an Elf hybrid and both his gifts and difficulties are typical of Elemental hybrids. Van Gogh could see and hear things that others could not, and these characteristics helped him to become a great painter. At the same time, he was mentally unstable. He had difficulty living as a human with the perceptions he continually experienced from the Elemental world.

Like other Elemental hybrids, he entered human evolution to learn free will and unconditional love. Van Gogh exerted his will in many ways, including his decision to take his own life. This was unfortunate, as Divine Law does not sanction suicide. Elf hybrids are attracted to ending their lives, and may do so because they do not wish to become old or lose their beauty or bodily functions. In the Elemental world, even when Elves are very old, they are still fully functional. This is very different than humans, who generally lose physical strength and other capacities with age. Van Gogh's life demonstrates many of the difficulties that occur when Elementals cross from elemental evolution to the human world and confuse the norms and laws of these two diverse evolutions.

All types of Elemental hybrids must guard against addictions. They can become addicted very easily—alcohol, drugs, cigarettes, sex, food, or a combination of all. The reason they seek mood-altering drugs is that they are so quickly bored. In the Elemental world, if you're bored with your environment or circumstances, you just think of another costume or another setting, and it appears! It can be very boring in the human world where this doesn't happen. Although all types of Elemental hybrids may have this problem, Elves and Leprechauns are especially prone to addiction.

There are two main kinds of Elves: Royal Elves and Forest Elves.

ROYAL ELF

Royal Elves are the ruling class of Elementals, and both male and female hybrids are most often beautiful and charismatic. They are usually tall and slender with classic good looks with lovely skin, flowing hair, large eyes, triangular-shaped face and sometimes even have slightly pointed ears.

If there were thirty people in a room, your eye would most likely be drawn to the Royal Elf hybrid. That would be someone who looks like two characters that David Bowie created. The first was Ziggy Stardust and the second character was the King of the Goblins in the film Labyrinth who carried the essence of a Royal Elf. Royal Elf hybrids are attracted to the arts, music, dancing, painting, acting, writing, and making stained glass. Creatively, they have enriched the human world more than any other hybrid.

Royal Elf hybrids often carry a sense of privilege, like to be taken care of and are unlikely to be the ones doing the dishes. They are charming, so you want to do something for them because you want to be liked by them. Elf hybrids are drawn to beauty and often do not look their age. They may not think so, but they are still beautiful in old age. Because of their physical beauty and how highly they value beauty in themselves and others, they often find it difficult to accept aging with good grace. Elf hybrids, especially Royal Elf hybrids, are androgynous and often bisexual, although they may not act on these inclinations.

Although I'm talking of the various difficulties and gifts of each of these hybrid evolutions, don't forget that they can learn to develop other gifts as well. A Royal Elf, for example, rather than just focusing on making herself beautiful, could create a beautiful home and cook wonderful food so people feel nurtured in her presence.

➤ Royal Elf Hybrid: DEVON

"I never really mastered the quantitative, acquisitive, mechanistic, and numerical way of humans. My mental metabolism is a bit slow, but my physical metabolism is very fast. Most people are surprised at my youthfulness. I think I'm a late developer, still waiting to grow up, not sophisticated in the ways of the world, but can appear so by acting and portraying different sub-personalities. There have been relatives in both my natal bloodlines that lived over a hundred years; my mother and her three sisters all lived over ninety years. I am somewhat androgynous and narcissistic, although matrimony has tamed me and made it safer for me to be in this world.

"From the earliest age, I have had an inordinate love and connection with nature and a deep sense of imminent transcendence in nature. I once played Ratty in Wind in the Willows; I had to lead Mole into a wood where Pan revealed himself and I had to portray awe before that deity. I was well chosen for the role. As recently as three weeks ago, while reading that section of the book to some friends, I broke down in a passion of hot tears while recalling this very powerful experience.

"I enjoy speaking and playing the piano, violin, and accordion in public. The main work of my life has been designing and making stained glass for public and private buildings, working directly with colored light—with actual (not depicted) light and darkness. Now I've just started producing pastel paintings as well."

✒ Royal Elf Hybrid: KEVIN

"I am mercurial, perceptive, penetrating, and creative in improvisation, art, music, and humor. Spiritually, I have a deep abiding awareness of my relationship with the Universe. Difficulties I have had that relate to my Elfin heritage are perfectionism, impatience, rebellious nature, and disdain for authority. The greatest lesson I have learned being a hybrid is to have compassion for the ponderous nature of people and to treasure my own nature."

✒ Royal Elf Hybrid: INGRID

"I am emotionally, mentally, and spiritually sensitive. I love beauty in nature and, as a child, collected nice stones that were my treasure. I built a cemetery for insects and buried them in little matchboxes for coffins, and made little gravestones and wood crosses. I spoke with different animals and plants. I built an altar for all the different seasons to thank Mother Nature for her gifts. I sat for hours in the swing, singing real and fantasy songs, and loved the world of fairy tales and myths and wanted to be a part of them. I felt like a little princess and dressed and behaved like one. I even cooked fantasy food with plants and herbs for people who were ill to help them recover.

"As a teenager, I liked to dress in a beautiful and extraordinary way, worked as a mannequin during my student years, and even won a beauty competition as the 'Most Beautiful Lady of Munich'. This was important to me until the age of fifty.

"I am creative, write songs, and love to play music and sing. My husband, also a Royal Elf, and I often have problems with other people because we protect nature against chemicals, pollution, destruction, and lovelessness. We have a big garden, speak with many spirits of nature (stones, plants, and different animals), feed, shelter, and protect animals. Even our cat and dog are really special and full of love for people and other animals.

"We have deep insights into the relationship between the spiritual and physical worlds. Out of this follows the question: What can we give back to the world for the gift of being born here on Earth? The greatest lesson we have learned as hybrids is to look into the different levels of the world, speak to the different spirits, and feel as an instrument of God and the spiritual world to help other beings."

FOREST ELF

Many things about Royal Elves apply to Forest Elves, including a tendency towards addictions. But there are also physical and personality differences between these two types of Elf hybrids.

Forest Elves tend to be a little shorter than Royal Elves and perhaps are not as charismatic. That's because in a forest you want to blend in and be camouflaged rather than stand out and be noticed like the Royal Elves. Forest Elf hybrids prefer to wear clothing in natural greens and browns. Nature is very important to them, so they enjoy organic gardening and tending trees. Forest Elf hybrids might also be drawn to acting careers, although not so interested in appearing beautiful as in camouflaging themselves in the characters they portray.

Forest Elf Hybrid: MOLLY

All Forest Elves that shared their stories spoke of their love of trees and forests.

> "I have been blessed to live close to nature for most of my adult life. Several times a week, I walk in the forest by my home, sit by the river, and pray for the wellbeing of Nature. Being in Nature is very important to me and I feel strongly about protecting it. When a flood in my city wreaked havoc with the forest outside my balcony, I wanted to hold the energy and space while Mother Nature recovered her equilibrium. Even though my building was evacuated for over a month, I would visit my condo regularly to sit and pray for a speedy recovery for the trees, animals, and plants.

➤ Forest Elf Hybrid: SEAN

"I love being creative, love plants and herbs, and love watching them grow. I have progressed to wild crafting, harvesting in harmony with the moon's phases. I like to be in nature, the woods especially (not really a beach person), and I like to be in the shade under a canopy, even in the rain. About twenty years ago, when I first came to Vancouver and didn't know many people here, I would take long walks alone in Stanley Park. One day I discovered an old tree stump. Well, 'stump' would be an understatement; it is the remains of a once magnificent tree. I call it 'First Cut' because if you look at it from one side, where the lumberjacks made a straight deep cut in its trunk to enable them to fell this tree, you notice the mark of their first cut has left a definite face outline on its bark.

"Anyway, a couple of times a year since then, I find myself in the park, sitting atop this slowly decaying stump, which is about twelve feet tall and at least fifty feet in circumference. First Cut is still there spiritually, watching the thin, newer, second-growth trees surrounding it as they grow. First Cut was obviously, by the size of its remaining stump, the largest tree of that part of the forest, and I sense that it is male, the father. I take it offerings of tobacco and sometimes coins. Strangely, my rituals do not seem odd to me, and time I spend there, no matter rain or shine, always recharges me.

"First Cut is not sad, and sometime it lets me see what it saw from its highest bow. It always reminds me of time and stability and the interconnectivity of things. Even though it is no longer the giant of the forest, it is still very much alive and a strong influence there."

*W*ell, I must admit Tanis did a crack-up job describing Elves in all their glory ... however ... I do have something to add! They can be a bit superficial and this presents a problem in the human world when they enter as hybrids. You humans fall for them right off, just like candy to a kiddy, but you are constantly disappointed when they leave you or don't follow through on their promise (unlike Leprechauns, I might add). Still, to be fair, the old Elves, Masters, you might call them, who enter your world do so to develop compassion, tolerance, forgiveness, and commitment. When they achieve these qualities, it is joy to behold and they make all Elementals proud of them. Now, back to my co-writer.

TREE DEVA

A nother interesting earth hybrid is the Tree Deva—the beings who live in trees and give them consciousness, much as human beings have souls that give them consciousness. The Druids spoke of sacred trees which they categorized as the oak, yew, hawthorn, and holly. In acknowledging their sacredness, the Druids acknowledged their evolved consciousness.

An old tree can be very wise. I once met a tree that was several hundred years old and I asked it, "What have you learned in these several hundred years?" The Tree Deva replied, "To stay in one place and learn all you need to know." Occasionally an evolved Deva of a tree may decide to enter human evolution. And why would an Elemental or a Tree Deva want to become human? Because humans are the creators on this planet and Tree Devas want to be full creators, which means learning to use free will as humans do.

Tree Deva hybrids are here to serve. Their priority is the health and harmony of the Earth and this is more important than any interest in humans. They are drawn to work in any field that helps the environment, such as recycling, cleaning rivers, and alternative power sources, such as wind and solar. However, their real gift is with trees. It is highly probable that Tree People, the non-profit international organization based in Los Angeles is comprised of Tree Deva hybrids, as their mission is healing trees, planting trees, and saving trees from being cut for lumber.

Because Forest Elves and Tree Devas are both interested in trees it might, at first glance, be difficult to determine the difference between these two kinds of hybrids. The key is service. Forest Elf hybrids want to learn free will and also to save the environment; however, their depth of commitment will seldom over-ride their own happiness or well-being. Tree Deva hybrids will be one-point focused on saving the planet at the expense of their health and relationships. Because of this, Tree Deva hybrids need to learn to preserve their health and find life balance and joy in the human world.

Lloyd again … I've got something to add here. Tanis is only talking about Tree Devas, but there are many more types of Devas. For a start, we've got Mountain Devas, Forest Devas who look after entire forests, and Ocean Devas. To Elementals, Devas are like your Angels. They are higher evolved than most Elementals in some ways and work directly with Spirit. Just like Angels can enter human evolution to help humans, Tree Devas, more than the other types of Devas, can enter human evolution to help the Earth.

✦ Tree Deva Hybrid: FIONA

"I feel like a tree, rooted deeply in Mother Earth, at peace when I am among trees. I even have long, large legs reminiscent of trees, and sexually, I enjoy physical touching as much as orgasm.

"I have always felt I was more of an outsider and, even today, am challenged by discussions that hold no meaning. It has been easier as I get older, most likely because I attract friends more similar to me. I live outside the mainstream. I have difficulty in crowded places, such as cities and in crowds of people, and am very sensitive to violence of any form, especially to animals. Also, I don't like deep water—being on a cruise is definitely not my ideal.

"Since my early teens, I have conversed with a higher power and this continues today in my daily conversations with Spirit. In my quiet places, I hear messages from the earth/spirit for myself and others. People are attracted to me as they experience me as a calm force. I listen and hold space for people to find themselves and to live their best life.

"My partner and I have developed our property, two-and-a-half acres including a grove, with the help of the Fairy energy that lives here. We share a healthy and happy co-existence of both sentient and galactic beings here. Visitors notice a significant shift in their energy once they cross our property line. Much of this is due to our intentionality, as well as the presence of hybrid energy."

HELPFUL HINTS FOR ELEMENTAL HYBRIDS

1. Be very careful about consuming addictive and/or mind-altering substances as you have a tendency to become addicted.

2. If possible, enjoy daily time in nature and consider living in the country, unless you are a Royal Elf hybrid, and then cities are fine for you.

3. Be alert to urges you have which do not conform to human standards, such as extra-marital affairs. Learn to pause before acting on these urges or you might find yourself in trouble.

4. You will find more happiness if you have a career which you believe is helping the environment or the Earth.

5. Remember that the two main reasons you have incarnated in human evolution are to learn love and to use your free will appropriately for the good of all.

SECTION 2:

HUMAN COUSIN HYBRIDS

The next category of hybrids has a common ancestor with humans. These include Inner Earthlings, Giants, Merpeople and Selkies, Dolphins and Whales.

INNER EARTHLINGS

In earlier times, when our planet was still shrouded in mist prior to Atlantis, there were many humanoid races developing here. One was a race called the Hyperboreans, known by many names in different cultures and mythologies that are often based on fact.

In Irish mythology, Hyperboreans are called the Fomori, sometimes anglicized to Fomorians, who lived in Ireland in ancient times. The Tuatha de Danaan, the race living in Ireland prior to the coming of the Celts, fought the Fomorians and defeated them.

In Greek mythology, these same Hyperboreans were referred to as the Titans, whom the Olympian gods of Greece fought against and defeated. The Olympian gods were the Atlanteans. When a later cycle in human evolution replaces an earlier one, the history of the earlier culture is often lost and demonized.

It's time for a bit of history about the Hyperboreans so you can more clearly understand the gifts they have, both as Inner Earthlings, where they live to this day, and also as hybrids who have entered human evolution.

At the time of pre-history hundreds of millions of years ago, when Hyperboreans were living on the surface of this planet, they lacked individuality and were mentally and emotionally more like animals. They were able to work with Earth elements in order to manifest bodies of various shapes and sizes. They experimented with building forms, like rocks, and helped to make our planet more solid. The statues and drawings of the Earth Mother, found in native cultures around the world, show her with exaggerated hips, stomach, and thighs, which represent the storage of power that Hyperboreans held in their lower bodies.

During that ancient time, the Sun increased the energy it sent to Earth and the mist began to burn off. When the mist disappeared, the Hyperboreans could no longer live on the Earth's surface, so they relocated inside the Earth and presently exist in a dimension other than the third-dimensional reality of which most humans are conscious.

The descendants of the Hyperboreans now live in the inner heart of the Earth and work with the evolution of the Earth's consciousness. Their evolution has gone along a different path from humans on the Earth's surface as these Inner Earthlings are developing other gifts. There was antipathy between surface and Inner Earth dwellers, so they separated.

Some Inner Earthlings have become hybrids to work more directly with humans and to assist humans in developing technologies in which they are highly knowledgeable. They are forerunners, preparing the way for the two races to meet again to work together in the future. As humans become conscious in the fourth and fifth dimensions (which is occurring now), they will become aware of the existence of Inner Earthlings and both races will work together for the betterment of other species on the planet. Their ability to reverse polarity allows beings from the Inner Earth to welcome UFOs to Earth, and one of their purposes is to act as traffic controllers for UFOs.

Unlike Trolls, who are amazingly strong and who love to work with stone, Inner Earthlings have powerful mental bodies they use to work with Earth elements. They are able to move stone mentally and showed the ancient Atlanteans, Egyptians, and Tuatha de Danaan how to do this in building their pyramids and stone circles. The foremost commitment, purpose, and unique qualities of hybrids from the Inner Earth are to assist in the evolution of the Earth as a conscious being. They have great knowledge of the mineral kingdom, including those unknown to humans. They encourage minerals and precious stones to grow much as humans grow children.

Inhabitants of the Inner Earth have a deeper understanding of the principles of time, space, and gravity than humans. As hybrids, they are interested in leading-edge inventions that better the planet, such as aromatherapy, tuning forks, lasers, and crystals. They are interested in solar, wind, waterpower, and alternative heating systems not widely spoken about in mainstream culture. In their own dimension, Inner Earthlings use telepathy, levitation, and advanced laws of magnetism and gravity to move themselves and others through time and space without machines.

Because the polarity of the Inner Earth is more negative (yin) than the positive (yang) charge of the Earth's surface, the talents of Inner Earth hybrids are more yin. They prefer to stay in the background and have a more introverted, hermit-like personality. Because of their gift with negative polarity, they are especially adept at working with the unmanifested world to bring what is unmanifested into form.

Spiritually, these Beings are quite advanced. Inner Earth hybrids might seek spiritual teachers and books that are concerned with Spirit. Some hybrids from Inner Earth have been monks or lamas in Tibet and other high mountain ranges.

Hybrids are usually fair skinned and may be bald or have thinning hair. For example, one hybrid I know has alopecia, a condition where one loses all body hair. The eyes of Inner Earth hybrids are very different from humans. Usually light in color, and sensitive to the light, almost as if they have no eyes, which is why they often wear glasses because of this. An albino is often a hybrid between this Inner Earth race and humans.

Inner Earth hybrids could happily live by themselves. They have a scholarly temperament and bond more with their books than with humans. A friend I've known for over forty years is an Inner Earth hybrid and he describes his talents as introspective, independent, and scholarly research with application to problems of life... "an observer of all things and no things."

I do not mean they lack love, as they are devoted to helping all beings on the Earth, but generally, they are not as personally devoted to individuals as other hybrids, and so form somewhat non-attached relationships. They are cautious of people and have good antennas for determining if others are trustworthy. They use this gift well.

*I*nner Earthlings visit our Elemental world as well as your human realm. We've even got our own ambassadors. In fact, whereas hardly any of you humans ever have contact with them, they are well known here and work with all castes, especially among us Leprechauns and Trolls. Elves often host them as well. I've worked with one over the years in studying the laws of magnetism and attraction.

Of course, I've got no trouble with that in my own world, but working with the human world which is so much denser, it's harder to get those laws working. My ambassador—I call him Sam because you'd never be able to pronounce his real name—has been especially helpful in showing me how to de-manifest in heavier realms so I can move Elementals from all areas of the Earth to work with humans in various places.

➤ Inner Earth Hybrid: JANICE

"I have had vision challenges since I was a young child and have worn glasses since age seven. My eyes are extremely sensitive to bright light. I used to trip and fall frequently. I cannot see well in the dark and need light to see where I'm placing my feet as I have anxiety about tripping and falling when I cannot see where I'm walking.

"I am not good at sports and never had an interest in participating in any sports. I do love to walk in nature, and can walk for miles if the terrain is relatively level. I am very sensitive to both heat and cold and have a low tolerance for either extreme—especially heat. My very fair skin can sunburn in a matter of minutes.

"Because I was extremely shy as a young person, I didn't start dating and exploring sexuality until I was almost twenty years of age. Although I wanted to be in a loving, committed relationship, this didn't happen until I was almost thirty, and it was my partner who taught me a lot about communication and being playful.

"I have always been extremely sensitive emotionally, with an ability to sense what others are feeling by observing their body language and the tone of their language—and just through sensing their energy. This sometimes became quite overwhelming and I didn't know how to deal with it so I spent a lot of time by myself. I found comfort spending time with the animals on the farm where I grew up.

"This was not always helpful as it made me feel isolated. Because I learned school subjects quite easily and did well on tests, I felt judged by fellow classmates as being one of the smart kids, which further isolated me. I tried to be invisible, so did not participate in school events or participate in group conversations.

"I loved reading, particularly about animals of all kinds, flowers, rocks, and how things were interrelated and interdependent. I also read anything I could find on the supernatural and extrasensory perception.

"I've always had a connection with a higher power and was raised in a family who attended church every Sunday. However, I experienced some incongruency with how I understood Christian principles and how people in my community and family treated each other. In my late forties, I felt a deep longing for something more meaningful in my life and began taking workshops about self-awareness and spirituality. I felt drawn to a spiritual path that was aligned to nature and reverence for the Earth. I had a wonderful opportunity to experience some native spiritual ceremonies and felt a strong connection with their honoring and respect for the Earth and her creatures.

"I feel my greatest lesson in being a hybrid is tolerance, respect, and gratitude for the diversity of life on our beautiful planet and how each life form has something to contribute to the whole. I have a broad overview of life and certain events. I'm often able to see and understand things that aren't visible to the mainstream population and have learned the importance of compassion and diplomacy."

HELPFUL HINTS FOR
INNER EARTH HYBRIDS

1. Because your nature is introverted, you may be tempted to withdraw from human interaction and become a hermit. Find a balance for life between your inner nature and the outer world.

2. Because you are committed so deeply to the Earth, you might be intolerant and impatient with those who are not. Practice compassion.

3. You might have a tendency to think you know more than others. There is some truth to this, but practice humility.

4. Because you take issues so seriously, you may need to lighten up, enjoy life, and develop your sense of humor.

5. Your talents may not be appreciated or your wisdom acknowledged, which may be frustrating. Recognize those who value you and be grateful for them.

GIANT

W hen most of the Hyperboreans moved to the Inner Earth, a few decided to adapt to living on the surface. Those who remained have taken two paths.

Some chose remote locations not frequented by humans so they could live in isolated groups. These became the Sasquatch (also known as Bigfoot) of North America and the Yeti of the Himalayas. These beings are stronger, larger, taller (usually between nine and twelve feet tall) and hairier than humans. They usually travel and forage for food at night when the heat of the Sun does not bother them. Their eyes are very sensitive to light and they are telepathic, as are their predecessors, so they communicate with each other and with humans through telepathy. The minds of Sasquatch are so strong that they are able to erase the memory humans have had of meeting them.

Contacts with Sasquatch increasingly are documented with video and audio recordings. Like the inhabitants of Inner Earth, they can be invisible to onlookers if they so desire, and they are able to move into another dimension where they cannot be seen.

I was fortunate to have an encounter with a Sasquatch in the Rocky Mountains of Canada, and thirty years ago, I remember hearing Dyhani Ywahoo, a well-respected Cherokee medicine woman, recount her experience with Sasquatch. She was in the forest at night and a Sasquatch family took her to their camp. You may ask, "Did this happen in the third dimension or in another one?" It could be either—or both. Just like with Elementals ... some people see them in the third dimension while others see them in the fourth.

The second group of Hyperboreans who remained on the Earth's surface decided to interbreed with the Atlanteans and their successors. They became Giants. In the Old Testament of the Bible, we hear of them when David killed the Giant, Goliath. Giants are prominently figured in Cornish, Welsh, and Breton folklore. In Ireland, the legendary hero Finn MacCool was said to have been a Giant. Even in the eighteen-hundreds, there were records of Giants living in North Antrim in Northern Ireland. Skulls found there were three times the size of an average human skull. I wrote in *Pilgrimage with the Leprechauns* that our tour was co-led by a Giant hybrid who spoke about the area where he grew up in Ireland as being famous for having Giants.

Giants were hybrids of the Hyperboreans who remained on the surface of the Earth. Hyperboreans who entered the Inner Earth became smaller and of average human size. Most of the true Giants have died out on the Earth's surface. However, as with albinos, sometimes there are throwbacks to these earlier times. It is more common for a Giant to be a hybrid in the human world today rather than be born a true Giant.

A Swedish friend of mine, Wanja Twan, is comfortable in publicly discussing her Giant-Neanderthal heritage. She has spoken to inhabitants in southern Sweden who claim to be descended from Giants. She believes that Giants may be related to Neanderthals and that Giants also are related to the Sasquatch. Interestingly, her husband devoted his life to searching for Sasquatch.

Wanja says, "In my family, my grandfather could lift a thousand-year-old oak tree that five men could not lift. He would spit on his hands and slap them together and you could see the sparks flying. Then he'd slap his hands again after lifting." Wanja continues, "I myself need very large shoes and can hardly find any that fit. I have a high tolerance for pain, a lot of stamina, and can focus on one thing for a long time. I like to lie for hours in cold water. Sasquatch also like the water. I love to be barefoot and lie outside at night. I have better night vision than normal, which is the same as Sasquatch, and don't need to put on lights or use a flashlight to see."

A Giant hybrid, like the Inner Earth hybrid, is likely to have an interest in books and learning about anything to do with the Earth and Earth healing. They do not like to take direction from others, being more of an "I'll do it my way" individual. They are usually larger and stronger than the average human and have larger heads. Giant hybrids often feel awkward in their body, as if it doesn't fit with all the little people around them.

They often feel unloved; remember that human myths have not been kind to Giants. Despite their large size, they are overlooked because unconsciously they try to make themselves smaller to fit in and not be intimidating. Their nature is to be gentle.

They need to learn to be proud of themselves and to find allies who love and appreciate them for exactly who they are. When they become more comfortable with humans, Giant hybrids will demonstrate their keen observance of others and the world around them, especially the natural world. Because they remained on the Earth's surface when their ancestors went to the Inner Earth, Giant hybrids are in many ways closer to humans than other hybrids.

Their gift is both inner and outer power. As hybrids they are most likely taller and bigger built than the average person and will be concerned that people respect what they have to say.

L loyd here AGAIN. Giants have never left our Elemental realm and we get on just fine with them. This is one of the major differences between you humans and us Elementals. We like the diversity of having many different kinds of beings and you humans want to get rid of everything and everyone who is not like you. Hit home there, didn't I?

Not all of our Giants are that bright, maybe because we didn't make them evolve to survive, but that's OK. Our kiddies love to play with them and sometimes our young males give them a bit of a hard time, feeling their oats and the like, chasing them about, but there are no hard feelings. Afterwards, our ladies take those hard-done-by Giants some good food—they're especially partial to honey—and it makes it alright till the next time.

↘ Giant Hybrid: ROBERT

Robert is comfortable thinking of himself as having Giant and Neanderthal genes and believes he might have Merperson heritage as well. He, like Wanja, is heavy-boned and with a very large head and heavy brows.

"Wow, are you ever tall! How tall are you?" I often hear some variation of this when I go out in public … in line-ups at stores or the bank, at parties, or riding the bus. At six-feet, four-inches tall, I'm easy to spot in a crowd. Such questions don't really bother me since being tall is looked up to in this society. People tend to think you make a good leader, are strong and smarter when you're tall. All of which are true, of course! As a possible Giant/Merperson hybrid, I have a superiority attitude that is often proved correct when I interact with some (lots of) other humans (smile).

"I never really felt like I fit in with society and most humans. I'm an introvert who prefers being alone most of the time … away from other humans, that is. But I'm never alone since there are always a plethora of wondrous beings to hang out with. Since I was a child, my passions and perceptions were different than most. I've always been a nature boy, fascinated with animals, plants, rocks, water, geography, and weather. I've always had a deep connection with Earth and all the beings here. Some of my best friends as a child were animals. And I'm now exploring my ability to telepathically communicate with other beings. Such connection brings me so much joy.

"Water and all the beings living in water always held a magnetic fascination for me. I feel I have Merperson heredity. I'm an underwater photographer/videographer and advocate for aquatic ecosystems. Whenever I've lived away from water, I didn't like it. I have a need to be near, on, and in water. I have to swim often to feel whole. Kayaking, canoeing, and sailing fill the need when I can't actually be in the water. I've hiked and climbed mountains with friends and inevitably found myself swimming in the tiny tarns with aquatic salamanders, or sticking my head under tumbling torrents high in the mountains to hang out with tailed frog tadpoles suctioned on to the rocks. For these reasons, I feel I have both Merperson and Giant heredity.

"Spirituality has also been a passion since childhood. I was a Christian minister for a while (with two degrees in theology) due to my passion for connecting with God and Creation and helping others to do so. Now my spirituality is much more open and no religious structure or dogma suffices. Working with ideas, philosophies, beliefs, and mythologies interests me, as do truly green technologies that utilize Earth energies. I'm an environmental activist, protecting the support systems for human life and speaking up for the wolves, salmon, trees, and rivers who have no voice in human politics, business, religions, or courts! I've even spent time in jail as a result.

"I cannot fathom the stupidity of this society that is hell-bent on destroying itself and Earth. It is pure greed to believe in the superiority of humans justifying our domination of all below us, whether lower on the social ladder or viewing forests, minerals, plants, animals, water, and wind as just raw physical resources for us to use up. I feel my spirit and soul have been incarnated many times in various physical forms on Earth. I feel very much at home here. I have no desire to leave Earth for the stars or some imagined heaven. Heaven is on Earth: We just need to realize that and consciously evolve as we weave spirit and physical form together."

HELPFUL HINTS FOR GIANT HYBRIDS

1. Recorded in your being is the memory that humans cannot be trusted, so develop compassion and forgiveness to help them.
2. You may be quick to anger or feel slighted. Don't take everything personally.
3. Stand tall and be proud of your uniqueness instead of trying to blend in.
4. You can get more bees with honey, so use charm and humor instead of accusation.
5. You have deep intuition, telepathic, and psychic gifts. No one can lie to you. These gifts will be appreciated in the near future by humanity.

MERPERSON

I t is commonly thought that there are four major races of humans: White, Black, Yellow, and Red. However, there is another race of human evolving on the Earth; one whose roots go back to the earliest times and whose story is found in our myths. This is the Green race and Mermaids and Mermen are its representatives.

In order to do justice to the hybrids of the Mer race, it is necessary to reflect on our collective myths about them. In Scottish and Irish folklore, the "merrow" are described as having a gentle, kind, and loyal nature. It is told that long ago, when the Milesians first landed in Ireland, Merpeople swam beside their ships in greeting. In Finland, it is said that Merpeople could grant wishes and heal sickness. They were known around the globe—from the Sirena of the Philippines to the Javanese Queen of the Mermaids, Nyi Roro Kidul. In West Africa, Merpeople were called the Mami Wata, the Jengu in the Cameroon, the Rusalkas in Russia, and in Greece, the Oceanids or Nereids.

Perhaps the most detailed account of the nature of the Merpeople is found in the histories of ancient Sumeria and Babylon, which state that in their early days, they were assisted by a wise being named Oannes—a human on the top half and a fish on the bottom half of his body. Oannes taught the humans on land to construct cities and establish laws, also to plant various grains and collect fruits. In short, he advanced their civilization. As he was amphibious, Oannes would not eat on land so retired each night back into the ocean. These traits give us clues about the Merpeople who still live among us as hybrids.

It was not an easy time in human evolution when some early humans decided to evolve on the land and others, who later became Merpeople, Dolphins and Whales, decided to go into the water. This decision took place over millennia and there has always been a strong bond between these evolutions and humans because of this. The story of Oannes goes back to Lemurian times when the Green race of humans lived in the Mediterranean waters in the Middle East, down the coast of Africa, and in the area that is now Southeast Asia.

Over millions of years, humans on land became stronger and more intelligent because of the gifts bestowed on them by the Green race and others. Merpeople lived mostly in the water, could breathe underwater, and had webbed hands and feet. On land, they were more vulnerable to attack, and being peaceful, they did not like conflict, which made it difficult to defend themselves. Although a few Merpeople decided to stay in contact with humans to teach them, the majority withdrew into remote regions where they would have no contact with land-dwelling humans.

Some Bedouin and Nubians, like Anwar Sadat, are hybrid descendents of this race. Sadat was known for overthrowing the British colonials to liberate his country, instituting a multi-party system of democracy in Egypt, and negotiating a peace treaty with Israel, which garnered him the Noble Peace Prize. Fundamentalist Muslims who objected to his peace policies assassinated Sadat.

His life story provides insights into certain qualities of the Mer and Mer hybrids. They are intelligent, charismatic, and of strong character. They can often be found in the military or fighting for human rights and peace. They are natural leaders, yet keep their secrets to themselves. They want to help humanity develop and are honest and keenly aware of unfairness.

My Iroquois friend, synchronistically named Oannes, was a Mer hybrid. He spent his teenage years living with his brother in a hole in the ground they had made in the Northeastern United States. They preferred this to living in their comfortable family home because they were learning to live in nature. After studying marine biology at university, Oannes was chosen by the U.S. Peace Corps to work in two capacities in the Philippines.

He lived with hill tribes in the mountains, wore a loincloth like them, and adopted their customs. These people had very little contact with civilization and Oannes introduced them, as best he could, to tools and attitudes they would need to succeed in the modern world. In his second role, he was in charge of a marine ecosystem where, as a professional scuba diver, he was skilled in assessing damage to the water and its inhabitants, and in attempting to preserve its integrity.

When Oannes returned to the U.S., he got into trouble with the government because, as a native Iroquois whose people lived in both Canada and the States, he refused to recognize the border and his passport was confiscated. After all he had done for his government, he felt betrayed and decided to no longer adhere to what he considered were unjust laws. Later, he took up arms to work with the people of Nicaragua to overthrow the tyrannical government. I saw him before he left for this mission and I have not heard from him since. He exemplified the Mer hybrid.

Some babies are born with webbed feet and hands. Occasionally babies are born with a more serious condition called sirenomelia, more commonly referred to as "Mermaid Syndrome". They have fused thighs, bladder/kidney problems, and are often without a very long intestine or rectum. Although they usually die within a few days of birth, they have been known to live to age ten. Sirenomelia and the other minor symptoms of webbing are physical reminders of earlier times when Merpeople swam happily in our oceans, rivers, and lakes.

Physically perfect Mer hybrids have other defining

characteristics. They may be very drawn to the water, loving to swim and submerge themselves. Mer hybrids seldom look their age, have a strong constitution, are seldom ill, and may die of heart problems. My father carried the blood of the Mer race and actually looked very much like Anwar Sadat. In physical appearance, my father resembled Arabic, Semitic, and even Native American people.

I believe I carry this bloodline. As a four- or five-year-old child, I remember lying underwater in wading pools, not breathing for a long time, looking up to the surface, and thinking, "I bet I could breathe underwater." I stopped myself from attempting this as I somehow knew this would not be possible in my present body. Instead, I contented myself with holding my legs together, as if they were joined, and moving underwater as a Mermaid would.

Just a few words. Tanis is talking about Merpeople—the Green race she calls it—incarnating into other human races as hybrids. Well, we've got our own relationship with Merpeople. Those of the Mer race have been especially good at helping our advanced water Elementals learn to work with the Earth element. Just as you humans need to learn to work with all elements to become enlightened masters, so do we Elementals. Because Merpeople are both land and water dwellers, they can help us with this.

Also, if advanced water Elementals, known as Undines, are applying to enter human evolution as hybrids, they need to work with Merpeople first to learn how to work with humans. Undines have more in common with Merpeople as they have a strong relationship with both water and land.

SELKIE

Selkies, found in Irish, Scottish, and Icelandic myths, are referred to as "people of the sea" in these cultures. Another branch of Merpeople, Selkies took a different turn in their evolution from the Green race, much in the same way as Inner Earthlings and Giants have a common ancestor.

According to myths, Selkies look like seals but can turn themselves into human form to live on land. Humans are attracted to Selkies and, although the females are often loyal spouses, they prefer to return to the ocean if given the opportunity.

I have had a few interesting experiences with seals. On one of my sacred site tours to England, I took a group of people to Tintagel, which is reputed to be King Arthur's birthplace. Tintagel is located on a bay. After our meditation, we had a little free time so I decided to walk along the beach. A seal came closer to shore and started calling me telepathically, "Come into the ocean, come into the ocean." I was not about to throw off my clothes and jump into the ocean in my underwear, so I refused. The seal called again, "Come on, come into the ocean to play with me." Once again, I said, "No."

Until then, the bay had been very tranquil, but suddenly a gigantic wave came out of nowhere and pulled me into the ocean to where the seal swam while laughing at me. As I dragged myself back onto the beach, with the seal still laughing, a guard who'd been watching the incident came running towards me. "I've been working here for twenty-five years," he said. "And we never get seals this close into shore. I have never seen anything like what just happened to you in all my life!"

I knew the seal that called me was a Selkie. They have a great sense of mischievousness, are very curious, and can often get themselves into trouble because of it. Selkies are shapeshifters and there is a kind of innocence about them, a lack of judgement sometimes. These qualities are very unlike the more serious and wise Merpeople.

I can't let the opportunity go by without a few words here. Selkies are real. They are as real as Merpeople WERE. The key is that Selkies have replaced Merpeople in the human world because the Merpeople have died out. Although, as I said earlier, Merpeople are still teaching Elementals in our dimension.

Some might say Selkies are degenerated, like Sasquatch are degenerated from the beings of the Inner Earth. I prefer to think that Selkies have their own gifts they are still bringing to the human world.

Both Selkie and Mer hybrids are living in the modern world and they share many characteristics. The one thing you humans would find to be different is that Selkie hybrids tend to be more dreamy and less focused than Mer hybrids. They have trouble getting their lives together sometimes. Lots of fantasies, but delivering the goods is not easy for them. That said, Selkie hybrids are not as angry as Mer hybrids can be. Mers love to stand up for a cause and you won't be finding that in Selkies.

Merperson Hybrid: JANINE

Robert, who recounted his story as a Giant, could easily have shared his story as a Merperson. Many people have the blood of the Mer race as well as being hybrids of another race because they carry one lineage from each parent. The following story is an example of a Forest Elf with a Mer heritage.

"I am so comfortable in water that I chose to live in river cities my entire adult life. Swimming and other water sports have been an ongoing life theme, contributing to both my health and pleasure. I deeply love to go to the sea, yet I do not live by the sea. I chose to live on the prairies, near the edge of the northern boreal forest. Since my early twenties, I have gone to the lake situated in this forest. I am strongly attracted to trees and must live with them around me. Every window of my house looks out at a beautiful tree.

"My mom and I share many characteristics, including a love of nature, both land and sea. My mom, one of her sisters, and her brother are long-time scuba divers and travelled to many reefs for diving. My mom even went on a dive to feed sharks! This is a hint about our Merperson heritage.

"I am kind of androgynous looking: small hips and breasts, broad shoulders, big back, muscular and lean, athletic. Never wear make-up or fussed much with my hair or clothing. I am very physically active and have maintained a high level of fitness throughout my life—an outdoor girl, a tomboy. I had a strong sexual drive up until my fifties. Learning to manage my sexuality has been an important lesson for me.

"I am a true introvert. I enjoy time alone, am a peacemaker, avoid conflict, and am stressed out by over-stimulation, crowded environments, too much responsibility, and extroverts. I am very secretive and private. I like to hide and blend in, observe and keep my thoughts to myself. I am a deeply caring person who finds fulfilment in looking after other beings—people, animals, plants. I have always felt somewhat separate from the rest of the world, somehow different. I do not have any close friends in the community I have lived in for over twenty-five years. I still feel like an outsider here … 'from away'. This does not trouble me.

"Nature has always been a direct link to Spirit for me. This is one of my clues that I have the Forest Elf in me. I could not live without the presence of nature in my life. It's hard for me to commit to Spirit in a big way because I am so attracted to the sensuality of this life. It's like my sensory experience of the world trumps my spiritual experience of this life. I'm working on giving more attention, time, and action to my spiritual body through meditation and yoga.

"Trying to blend in has kept me from achieving some goals. I've not stepped into my power in order to keep relationships intact (so I can go on looking after someone). My secretive nature has sometimes caused pain for me or another person. I have not been able to sustain any job for more than a few years—had lots of different jobs, workplaces, and career paths. This has resulted in financial instability. I think this could be my need for variety, coupled with my fiercely independent (and secretive) nature. I just prefer to do things my own way. Period.

"Self-employment as a yoga teacher has been such a blessing. My life as an adult has been a bit chaotic when I compare it to others who have the same job, career, spouse, home, community, etc. for their entire lives. I am comfortable and happy with very little stuff. I live in a small house with simple furnishings, few clothes, and all functional.

"Gifts that I think are typical of my Elf/Mer hybrid nature are that I am a peacemaker and protector of the meek. I make anywhere I live bloom by creating gardens and looking after the growing things. I nurture others and cultivate their gifts. I share my gift of physicality with others through teaching yoga and other movement classes. I am a student of dance because I love the beauty of this art form. I look after nature by living green, being a vegetarian, and caring for the living beings in my yard. I live a life of moderation so I leave a smaller footprint on the body of the earth.

"The greatest lessons I have learned being a hybrid are committing to something and someone and looking after myself."

HELPFUL HINTS FOR MER AND SELKIE HYBRIDS

1. Being charismatic, people are drawn to you. They trust you, while you do not trust others nearly so easily. Allow yourself to trust worthy individuals.

2. You are a warrior for peace and must learn to put aside the old physical weapons that were used on your race and employ the new ones of right speech and persuasion that are the weapons of the Aquarian Age. This is the time of the "water bearer"—when your skills, those of Merpeople, are most needed on the Earth.

3. You feel betrayal too keenly and must learn forgiveness above all else.

4. Sometimes you hide your skills to stay safe. It is time to step forward again.

5. Bring water into your life by living near water, swimming regularly, and having a fountain in your home.

DOLPHIN

Dolphin hybrids are one of the most common human hybrids. It is a relatively easy transition for Dolphins to enter human evolution as land-dwelling hybrids, because Dolphins and Whales are our human cousins who, during early Lemurian times, went into the sea to continue their evolution.

Many Mediterranean cultures believe that knowledge was brought from the Pleiades by Dolphin-like beings who breathed air, lived in the water, and had fish-like tails. These creation stories are also found amongst the Dogon of Africa and the Uros Indians who live on Lake Titicaca in Bolivia. Pleiadians have helped to create Dolphin evolution on Earth, and Dolphins are the yin part of the human race—that which brings grace, compassion, gentleness, and beauty.

The ancient Greeks called Dolphins the "people of the sea". Dolphins still have the bones for hands and limbs that are found in land-dwelling humans. Humans judge intelligence based on 1) the complexity of the brain and 2) the brain size per body weight of the being. Based on our own way of evaluating intelligence, Dolphins appear to be at least as intelligent as humans, because their brain is more complex and as large per body weight as that of humans. Their brain is very different from most land mammals, and although they do not have hair, they have hair follicles derived from their early land evolution. Dolphins are not animals—they are our cousins.

Like humans, Dolphins have unique personalities, and they exhibit many of the same qualities as humans. Individual Dolphins, like individual humans, are at different stages in their evolution. For example, the males sometimes fight with each other or try to kick other males out of the pods. Sometimes they will kill other species, such as porpoises, even when they do not eat them or there is no competition for food. Some Dolphins commit infanticide and males have been known to kill their own babies, or the babies of other males, so that the female will mate with them.

Both Dolphins and humans who engage in these behaviours are not very spiritually evolved and it is usually the more spiritual Dolphins that enter human evolution as hybrids. Some Dolphins in marine parks and zoos are actually "bodhisattva" Dolphins who live in the situation voluntarily to help humans learn to recognize the importance of all species and all life.

Dolphins, like humans, live in communities, where individuals may leave one pod to join another. Sex may occur among members of different pods, which is better for genetic diversity. As mentioned earlier, they are also known to interbreed with other Dolphin species, much like humans breed with members of other races and the Wolphin, a cross between a False Killer Whale and a Bottlenose Dolphin, is one of the results.

Dolphins, like humans, need to sleep and dream, but Dolphins in the wild sleep with one eye open. They have the ability to keep one brain hemisphere active, while the other hemisphere sleeps, so they can watch for predators. Dolphin hybrids might be able to teach humans this level of mind control.

Intuitively, we sense that Dolphins can register our emotions, zap energy blocks, and loosen any accumulation of negative energy we have. When they do this to us, our thoughts and emotions decrease. Our energetic field becomes calmer and more relaxed and open to higher levels of consciousness. Dolphins can heal autistic children by helping them to communicate. They can even diagnose illness in people. I know of one woman who was swimming with the Dolphins when one of them continually touched a place on her breast with its nostrum. She thought it was strange, but when her doctor examined her, breast cancer was discovered in that specific area.

Dolphin hybrids will often be attracted to healing professions and feel drawn to help those in physical, emotional, and spiritual need. One male Dolphin hybrid I know has been a Reiki Master for over twenty years and also one of the first individuals to use brain equipment to measure and change brain states for healing.

Brain research shows that when we swim with Dolphins our brainwaves slow down to the theta (dream) state. It is in this particular brain state that our thoughtforms were programmed during our early childhood. When we entrain to this brain state, the Dolphin's energy merges with our consciousness and magic begins, for it is in this state that our thoughtforms and bodies are able to heal.

Swimmers report miraculous results after spending time with Dolphins. People feel a state of bliss, often known as Dolphin drunkenness. Others report increased states of happiness, peace, release of physical pain, decreased addictive desires, increased creativity, decreased depression and anxiety, and a recharged immune system; and some report a deep connection with Spirit.

If you have swum with the Dolphins—as I have on several occasions—it's an incredible experience to see the profound, even human, intelligence emanating from their eyes. One Dolphin hybrid recounts her first time of swimming with Dolphins in the wild, "Time stopped. My thoughts ceased. I lost sense of self and time, as I floated along with the Dolphins below. Where they led, I followed. Their energy and the warm turquoise waters carried me along into the world of Presence, ever mindful, yet without mind. As I emerged from the depths of the ocean, I sensed my heart burst open with love that was beyond all limitation. I smiled. I cried. I had nothing to say.

There was no need for words. I felt only love."

There are many recorded instances of Dolphins saving swimmers from drowning and shark attacks. Dolphins are even known to assist other species. An example is Moko, a New Zealand Dolphin, who helped a Pygmy Sperm Whale and her calf out of shallow water when they were stranded.

Dolphin hybrids may likewise be drawn to help other species and one of their gifts is to go to the source of a problem and find a solution.

Dolphin hybrids have qualities that are often more developed than the average human. For example, they are more yin than yang. They are very sensual and enjoy beautiful clothes with soft fabrics and lovely colors, and to surround themselves with sensual delights. In this aspect, they are like Royal Elf hybrids. Dolphin hybrids love to be touched and to feel water and nice creams on their body.

Dolphins in the wild enjoy sex frequently and that can be difficult for Dolphin hybrids if they don't have a sexual partner with whom to enjoy touching and sex. Dolphins and hybrids alike may engage in homosexual, as well as heterosexual, acts and may become sexually active early in life. Unlike with humans, sexual guilt does not seem to be a problem for Dolphins, however it can become a big issue for Dolphin hybrids who may be ashamed of their sexual nature.

Dolphin hybrids love to play with others and prefer this to playing alone. Because they are warm and welcoming, others are drawn to them, and they enjoy a wide circle of friends and often belong to many different communities and groups. They are loyal and commit to long-term friendships, but because of their yin nature, they may be changeable. Their desire to experience everything may disperse their energy and confuse them, so they have difficulty following through on their goals and commitments. But they are easy to forgive and you cannot hold a grudge against a Dolphin hybrid because they exude love and compassion.

As with the other hybrids, it might be helpful to think of individuals you know with Dolphin hybrid qualities. For me, women like the late Marilyn Monroe come to mind. I am not saying that she is a hybrid, but the physical look, long-term friendships, and difficulties that she had with men, who loved and then abandoned her, are similar to those encountered by Dolphin hybrids.

I have something to say about Dolphin hybrids. Like the Merpeople, some of them have come into our world to help Elementals, not so much the water Elementals, but land-based ones ... Elves especially. You see, Elves can be a bit flighty and not as able to hold their own when they enter your human world as hybrids. So, advanced Dolphin hybrids, having learned how to keep on track in the land-based human world, teach Elves how to stay focused on a goal.

➤ Dolphin Hybrid: MARINA

"I love to be in the water and under the water. I feel excited and alive. I feel a sense of peace and at-oneness with my environment. If I am feeling unhappy or out-of-kilter emotionally, being in the water restores me. I love the feeling of cool water on my skin and the freedom of movement. I know that Dolphins are highly social, but my experience in the water is often a very personal, present in the moment, in the here and now experience and is solitary. I feel at ease, unobserved and so unselfconscious, hence this deep feeling of peace and joy. I feel my heart expanding as the cool clear water caresses my body.

"Water is denser than air, therefore it hugs the body, exciting the nervous system and heightening the sensuousness of touch. I love the feel of movement through water, the way the body is suspended and supported by it; the oneness of being embraced and surrounded in and by water.

"I came into puberty early, was sexually innocent, yet interested. There was some minimal early exploring, which later led to feeling shamed. I must say I liked boys, and on the whole, they liked me. I was fun, playful, flirtatious. Touch is important to me. It goes right to my heart and there is often a longing to have physical closeness in a sexual or sensuous way, although it is not without scruples. If I had the freedom to explore with whomever I was drawn to, that could be fun. It is not the desire to be with anyone and everyone, but to feel joy and happiness and the fun of sensuousness, the fun of relating. I like the lightness of being that comes with playfulness.

"I tend to be fairly subjective and personal. Impersonal people can throw me off. I am friendly, compassionate, caring, flexible, genuine, and strive to be honest. I do a lot of sensing by 'feeling' a room, for instance, and I have a big desire to help even the energy in the room. If someone is upset, I want to help him or her find peace. I am drawn to do what I can to stir up or to lighten the energy with humor and to bring harmony. When I am alone too much, I can feel depressed and lonely. I like to be with other people, but also need some time alone to metabolize what I have experienced and to know what I feel … to find myself. I spend much time sensing and feeling and then can be depleted or overwhelmed. I am a pretty constant person. I am curious and like to explore. Family and friends are important to me.

"I am drawn to the healing arts and my work involves hands-on bodywork. It also involves being with and aware of others; a coming together physically, emotionally, mentally, and spiritually.

"Although I am strongly emotional, I am also excited by ideas, like to read good literature, and to develop clear, rational thinking. I am aware and intuitive and, at times, fast thinking and acting. In other instances, I can be more ponderous, slow thinking and speaking. I really want to understand, but too much detail can drive me crazy. I want to get to the core of things and get there quickly.

"I like the idea of co-creating with others, of developing individually, but also to swim with a school of like-minded people. I am drawn to the high frequency of joy and laughter and like to be aware on an energetic level. I am thinking of the radar of Dolphins as they swim together. They hold a distance between each other as they zoom about jumping, thrusting, flipping, surging, adjusting, dancing through the water, moving as one, but also individually. They are aware and alive in their own skin. They have freedom of movement. I like to be with the whole as I am in my own skin, feeling my feelings, having my experience. I am part of the whole, of the unity."

Dolphin Hybrid: DONNA

"I always want to live by, or have a view of, water and I feel safer by or in the water. I feel moved by beautiful and graceful physical bodies. I love my body and dressing my body beautifully! I am constantly aware of my physical surroundings and notice the harmony or disharmony of it, i.e., lines, color, texture, shapes. My friends tell me my greatest gift is my expression of beauty and grace. "I feel more grounded when I have sex. Sexual intimacy feels natural and playful to me. I love touching and being touched sexually. I am sensitive to alcohol, cold, wind, mind-altering substances, violence, and dishonesty. I have tears when I know the Truth of something. I engage in relationship and with concepts, through connection and co-creativity with another person or the field of ideas. I truly want to know LOVE in my more intimate relationships. Beauty and flow in nature move me to feel connected. I feel Oneness with the water or the physical sun. When I dance and move to music, I open to spiritual clarity."

HELPFUL HINTS FOR
DOLPHIN HYBRIDS

1. Because you are a natural healer and warm-hearted, others are drawn to you and trust you. Learn discernment as people are not always what they seem and may prove untrustworthy.

2. Your sexuality and sensuality are beautiful. Bring the yin, feminine gifts into the human world in all your glory.

3. Play, play, play. It is a large part of your nature and something you can give to the human world that humans need.

4. Living near water is important for your physical, emotional, and spiritual health.

5. You intuitively pick up lack of harmony in others or in a situation and want to solve it. Sometimes the solution lies beneath your consciousness, so relax and let all come to you.

WHALE

Whale hybrids are more rare than Dolphin hybrids, although Whales are also "people of the sea" who left land evolution at approximately the same time as Dolphins.

Whales have a complex evolution, based on the collective rather than the individual focus of the Dolphin. This is why when one Whale beaches itself, the whole pod may choose to commit mass suicide and beach themselves as well. People have attempted to get Whales off the beach, only to find they would return and beach themselves again.

Whale hybrids are drawn to the collective group needs. Land-based humans may arrogantly think that individual evolution is more evolved than group evolution, but that's not so. Group evolution, such as that of Whales and Bees, teaches interdependence. The main gift Whale hybrids give us is the power and intelligence of the group.

Whales have a very complex communication system in that each Whale has its own unique name for itself. Not only can they communicate thoughts and ideas to one other, but captive Whales have been known to mimic human speech, demonstrating how they may be trying to communicate with us. Humpback Whale songs can last for thirty minutes, and are at such a low frequency, that humans cannot hear them.

Humans do not always hear everything Whale hybrids communicate either, as much of their communication is at the deep feeling level. Whale hybrids think if you were really interested in them, you would know telepathically how they are feeling without them having to express it.

Most Whales spend approximately ninety percent of their lives underwater, so very little is known about them. Many species travel great distances every year bringing information from the northern to the southern waters of our planet. Whales hold the collective unconscious for humanity. Whale hybrids are often deep-sea divers, bringing unconscious knowing back to surface consciousness. This is their gift to humanity, to the Earth, and to all Earth species. Whale hybrids carry ancient memories in their bodies of the Earth's past and the past of all races.

One of the difficulties that Whale hybrids may have is living alone and making their own decisions. They yearn to be part of a bonded group. They might also be a bit dreamy and go into their own world, even as Whales do when they dive hundreds of feet down into the ocean to commune with Spirit. Whale hybrids are usually deeply spiritual, psychic, and in tune with the harmony of Spirit, although they may not speak of this directly.

Whale hybrids do not need to lead but, depending on upbringing and parentage, may do so. They are also content to steer others from behind and are happy to let others shine. It is important to them to be with those who are making changes in the world, so they can share their observations. They are private and guarded about their own needs and feelings, but they may be healers in helping others explore their deep-seated issues to find solutions.

Whale hybrids often have problems with weight as they naturally have larger, well-padded bodies that protect them from the thoughts and feelings of others. This does not mean they are physically unfit.

Interestingly, Humpback Whales have been known to live into their seventies, and Bowhead Whales can live over one hundred years; life-spans that are naturally similar to humans. Living to a good age is true also for Whale hybrids, unless their hearts are broken. Because they feel everyone and everything so deeply—probably more than any other hybrid—their hearts are very tender and they feel rejection keenly. Whale hybrids need to learn to protect themselves from caring too deeply about what others think of them. Whale hybrids are capable of being fully independent, still, co-creating with others and devotion to others and the Earth is their main focus.

I haven't got a lot to say about Whale hybrids—now that might surprise you—because their great gift, as Tanis has said, is being able to carry the ancient memories of the Earth and to bring those memories back to your human consciousness. This might sound like bragging; nevertheless, Elementals can read the history of all the Earth and every human as easily as Whales. This is all recorded in what you folks call the Akashic Records in the astral world and, because Elementals live in a lighter frequency than you folks, we can "read" these records in an instant. It doesn't take any effort—it just is.

You will remember that Elementals evolve more in clans, and we are not as individualized as humans. In that way, we are more like the Whales. For this reason, both Elementals and Whales—as well as the hybrids of both species—feel more linked to the collective and are more in tune with the unity of all beings than are most humans. Both our species believe in co-creation and want to partner with others who wish to co-create a beautiful world, and that goes for hybrids as well.

➤ Whale Hybrid: PATRICIA

"From about the age of eight, I developed a weight problem. My weight and belly fat fluctuated from then on, but it was always a struggle to lose weight and keep it off. While I was influenced by social expectation to look good, I never felt an internal drive to be slim and trim. None of the self-help books or other explanations of my problem seemed to ring true. Fortunately, I am very healthy—even through a period of morbid obesity, my cholesterol and blood pressure were OK. Now I exercise an hour or two a day and eat a healthy diet—and still wear large or extra-large sizes, although I am 80 pounds lighter than a few years ago.

"Physically, I am active but never athletic. Heights and activities requiring sure-footedness bother me. I enjoy sex, especially when there is a deep bond of love and safety, but I have never been sexy or had much sexual fire. Emotionally, I am interested in flow, inclusion, interconnection, steadiness, deep emotional consciousness, insight, and intuition. I am very extraverted and optimistic, but I also need solitude and to go deep within myself and with other people. I get really bored by superficial discussions, trivia, etc., and only find patience when in the role of helper.

"Ancient and universal truths are extremely important to me. I am not an original thinker, but am very gifted at knowing when information or ideas have a truth or insight that needs to be shared. I take it in, then express the bridge from theory to application. Teaching and coaching people to open to their own truths and to universal truths—especially regarding interdependence and oneness—are

very important to me. I have always been a seeker. The
new emphasis on wisdom teachings brings me joy and
fulfils a deep need for affirmation of my own knowing.

"I feel like an old soul, yet everything is still new
and fresh to me. I was raised in a Protestant church and
was active until college, when I rejected creedal religion,
moved to humanist, and then later found transpersonal
psychology. Visiting ancient standing stones and spiritual
retreats, combined with intentional energy work, opened
me to a keener awareness of my spiritual depth and inner
life. I let go of my high achievement and strategic approach
to life for a gentler path of service through first being, and
then doing. Embracing the Divine Feminine, and working
to help people balance the male and female energies within
and around them, is at the heart of my spiritual work.

"I had an amazingly nurturing, child-centered start in
life. Like in Whale pods, I had a very close relationship
with my mother and was the golden child of our extended
family. I was never able to replicate that sense of total
acceptance, love, and support again. Individualization and
separation had to be intentional for me to grow. I often
tried to be both what my family wanted and expected, as
well as who I was meant to be, and so demanded a lot from
myself. Learning and finding that the love and support I
need is from the Universe, not mortals, was big for me.

"I have been blessed with a life of simple abundance,
unconditional love, and gifts that have allowed me to live
a life in flow. So far, I have had the insight to learn from
gentle prompting and seldom have had to be hit over the
head. I feel very guided and secure. Only in listening to
others' stories and hearing their pain, did I learn that not

everyone started with the unconditional love that provided me with a high sense of self-love and self-worth. I am grateful and committed to being a change agent because of this understanding. My gifts are excelling at group process and facilitation, interpersonal communication, deep listening, teambuilding, and having an ability to help people with life skills and transpersonal transformation.

"Having said that, I always wanted to fit in, but have never quite done so. I used to yearn to belong to a group, but could not find a peer group. I outgrow people and relationships very fast. My major difficulties have been: not getting credit for things I have initiated, having a deep knowing that seeks expression, but not always finding the catalyst to open myself to it, longing for a soul mate and soul family and accepting that this will not happen, to detach from this, and trust that the Universe will provide love and support.

"The hardest lesson for me was learning non-attachment. While I pursued my own truth and path, I longed for the depth and quality of connection I had experienced as a child. This led to very high expectations, disappointment and a feeling of aloneness that left me sad until I learned to live my own life, trusting that connection would come and go as needed, but that relationships are never permanent. What better reason to follow our own path is there than the realization that we come into this life from a myriad of different places and in different ways —yet we are all one."

HELPFUL HINTS FOR
WHALE HYBRIDS

1. You will seldom be recognized for the great being you are. Get over it and get on with being it.

2. Do not try to change your body shape to conform to Vogue's current standards. You are not an Elf. You are a Whale.

3. You are a deep seer tuned into the Earth's rhythms and, as such, you are a gifted healer who can help individuals uncover their unconscious and move them towards consciousness.

4. Your life is dedicated to service. That is why you have entered human evolution, but do not lose yourself here.

5. You may have difficulty communicating the depth of your "knowing" in words. Just realize that your feeling body is so strong that others pick up what you are sending through their feeling body.

SECTION 3:

STAR BEING HYBRIDS

Our last category of hybrids is the various kinds of Star Beings who have come to Earth to assist humans and other Earth beings with their evolution. These include Angel, El, Horus, Pan, Dragon, Bee, Centaur, and Anunnaki.

With the exception of the Anunnaki and sometimes the Angels, all other races in this section came to Earth as full Creators to help humanity become Creators. In the process, those who came and stayed have entered human evolution as hybrids, and so have lost the knowledge of their original heritage. Fortunately, many Star Beings still have the defining characteristics that will help them, as hybrids, to evolve back to full Creators.

ANGEL

Angel hybrids are one of the more common hybrids and are the largest group of hybrids that do not come originally from Earth. Many entered races as hybrids in other solar systems to help the inhabitants become conscious, much as they are helping Earthlings.

Angel hybrids become full Creators by entering human and other evolutions where they learn to develop free will. The function of Angels—in their original form—was to always do the will of the Creator; not have free will. Cosmic Intelligence has created multitudes of evolving beings in many solar systems; Angels help all of these evolving races to develop consciousness.

Angels are found in all religions, including Christianity, Islam, Judaism, Buddhism, and Zoroastrianism. Throughout history, individuals have related encounters with Angels. Right up to the present day, even in the mainstream, individuals trust and believe in Angels more than any other Star race.

This is one of the major reasons why Angels decided to enter human evolution as hybrids. They knew humans trusted them, and they wished to serve the cosmic plan in whatever capacity was needed. Their incentive to become hybrids was less of wanting to develop free will for themselves, which is the incentive for most hybrids, and more of wanting to be of service.

An important characteristic of Angel hybrids is their good hearts. There is something in them that attracts others ... people feel they are a better person if an Angel hybrid is in their life.

They have so many different gifts and talents that they can be found doing various kinds of work. This aspect of wanting to commit to and be loyal to Spirit is essential to their nature, even if they are leading a somewhat reckless life, i.e., sexual exploits, drugs, and other indulgences. Unlike Elemental hybrids, they seldom become addicted to any of these substances and usually by middle age, maybe earlier, find themselves increasingly drawn to Spirit.

My common-law spouse is an Angel hybrid. He exhibits the radiant qualities that both men and women are drawn to and they feel loved in his presence. Here's an example of how this works in life. For his sixtieth birthday, I gave him a party. He's a real manly kind of guy who loves fishing and tools, and the men at the party encircled him for the first hour. I suggested he might want to visit with his women friends, as they love him as well, and he went to the kitchen at my suggestion. Within five minutes, the men had followed.

Angels live within a hierarchy where there are stronger, older Angels, and younger, less experienced ones. The note of hope, for example, will be the same note of hope from a young or an old Angel. The only difference is that the young Angel does not have as much power as the older one, so the strength to affect a situation or person is greater for the older, stronger Angel ... the same way a larger bell can strike a more powerful note than a smaller one, and can be heard further away by more people.

Angel hybrids, like Angels, recognize their place and are not competitive to make themselves bigger than they are. Yet, they will stand up to be acknowledged for the gifts they have. They are happy to work selflessly for someone or an organization they feel is worthy of their efforts. They do not need to lead, although they are comfortable with the role, if their talents are obviously greater than the others. They serve the whole in whatever function is of most benefit to others.

Individuals such as the writers Louise Hay and Doreen Virtue have both written wonderful healing books about Angels that serve to bring Spirit's message to the world.

Angels on the various Rays of Energy have different qualities: peace, hope, healing, love, will, or fighting evil, for example. When you pray for help, an Angel who is the quality you prayed for comes to your call. So if you pray for healing, an Angel of Healing responds. If you are fearful and pray for peace, you receive an Angel of Peace.

I mention this because a great number of Angel hybrids tend to be on the Ray of Will. Archangel Michael, who is head of the Ray of Will, is a warrior Angel who goes wherever there is darkness to bring light. He is also a great protector of the weak and less fortunate, the guardian of humanity, and committed to helping restore us to the Cosmic Plan. It could be that Warrior Angel hybrids are needed more on this plane of material existence, and also that they have a strength—an inner determination—that may be missing in Angel hybrids with other talents.

All Angel hybrids develop their free will when they enter human evolution. Most become very interested in developing themselves in any way they can. But first, they want to help others and look for opportunities to do this.

Mother Mary had many qualities that one might find in Angel hybrids, as did Jesus. Their purity, devotion to serve the Divine Will, and courage to undergo any tests are characteristics of well-developed Angel hybrids.

Angel hybrids feel they must serve Spirit and, when they don't, they are consumed with fear, anxiety, and guilt. They may feel they are not good enough and have not done enough. This comes from having once been so pure that they made no mistakes. These hybrids must give up guilt and realize that the human path of evolution is one of trial and error.

In relationships, Angel hybrids can have extremely high standards for their partner because they are well aware of what is perfect. Let's face it, few of us on this Earth are perfect—or we wouldn't be here! Angel hybrids must learn to bring the same compassion they have for the masses of humanity they are trying to help into their personal relationships.

Spiritually, Angel hybrids may be more attracted to "bhakti", which is devotional yoga, as their strength is their devotion to a spiritual teacher as a representative of Cosmic Intelligence.

L loyd here. Devas in our Elemental world do most of the things that Angels do in yours. They oversee our evolution and keep us aligned to Spirit's path if we stray. Our Old Ones do this too. That's not to say we don't have any Angels coming to our world. We are well aware of Mother Mary and Jesus the Christ, and most of the evolved ones in your human world have spent some time with us, mostly coming when we call, as opposed to living with us. That's because to be a full Creator on Earth, you need to be able to work with all kingdoms of creation.

Still, it's mostly our Old Ones who work with Angels who keep them informed of the evolving Cosmic Plan, rather than Angels working with individual Elementals. I'm just now at the stage where I'm getting to see more of this, but not enough that I feel qualified to speak.

➤ Angel Hybrid

When I asked people I knew to write their stories about the hybrid that they think they are, more Angel hybrids responded—and quicker—than any other type of hybrid. Psychologically, many of us would prefer to be an Angel because of their positive reputation with humans.

Many Angel hybrids feel connected to Archangel Michael, the Warrior Angel.

ANN: "Injustice is one thing I cannot tolerate and I will fight to defend someone, or something, being mistreated."

MATILDA: "My work pulls me into dark areas when working with people with trauma—whether in shelters, treatment centers for addictions and mental illness, poverty, immigration, aboriginal students—often coming from a lot of deep pain."

JENNY: "As the oldest girl in a large family, I assumed responsibility early in life while fighting all the family dysfunction. I felt it was up to me to protect my siblings and get them out of a difficult situation. I think this was often perceived as being bossy."

SAM: "I am passionate about protecting family and friends and expect the same in return. I hate quitting and my will to continue with a job/responsibility/challenge is quite strong."

Several of the Angel hybrids are physically stronger and more muscular than the average person, while a few are weaker and of average build.

ABIGAIL: "I chose a very strong, sturdy, healthy body for this incarnation, and good thing because I've needed it. I've had to do an inordinate amount of physical labor and have the strength to do it. With blonde hair and blue eyes, I look like many people's idea of what an Angel hybrid might look like, and it was even more pronounced when I was a child."

SAM: "I have a very dense body composition. I have always weighed twenty-five to forty pounds more than most people would guess. I am physically very strong and have a larger-than-normal head. I was very athletic in my youth and usually the best player on every team."

JENNY: "I seem to require some weight on me. I thought I was just overweight, but I think it's more than that. It's like I need a protective 'buffer' to shield me from the negative energy around me."

Angel hybrids all recounted that they feel things very deeply.

DEBBIE: "I'm not very sturdy emotionally. I cry easily when frustrated."

MATILDA: "I let people walk on me before I fight back. My role is to serve, so it is hard for me to distinguish when people are using me."

JENNY: "I am very sensitive both to my emotions and to the emotions of all those around me. I can feel the pain and suffering in others and it breaks my heart."

ABIGAIL: "I feel deeply for others' suffering and always, always want to help them alleviate their suffering in one way or another. I am very compassionate, empathetic, impassioned about justice, truth and love for all, and see all humans living as brothers and sisters around the Earth."

Many Angel hybrids signal their weak area as being perfectionism.

TROY: "I feel pressure to deliver on my role, and anxiety that I am not doing it ... or doing enough ... or worst case ... doing the wrong things out of poor understanding of the assignment."

JENNY: "A perfectionist trait has followed me all my life; I'm still that way. I always set high standards for myself (and others) and I'm always disappointed because I fall short of meeting them. I'm very good at beating myself up."

A few hybrids mention their tendency to project their desire for perfection on their partners.

GABRIELA: "In my first marriage, I expected my spouse to be perfect (an Angelic version of perfection, that is!). I spoke to him often, trying to convince him that life could be perfect if only he... He later came to refer to me as 'holier than thou!'"

Angel hybrids have a deeply spiritual nature from an early age.

MATILDA: Has a postgraduate degree in Divinity; "I have always been spiritual, even as a small child, and I always wanted to do God's Will."

ANN: "My life is not my own; it belongs to the Creator. The Bible talks about being "A servant of the most high" —well, that's me. I can't help myself; it's not only what I do, but also who I am. I've been sent to help many through the hardest times of their lives. I rarely know what I'm getting into until I'm there and bit-by-bit, it unfolds. As I follow Divine guidance, everything works out perfectly. Whatever is needed is what I do."

DEBBIE: "I live with my cup overflowing and love to share it with others. I am an optimist and consistently engage others in gratitude and appreciation for life and all it serves up!

"It makes me so sad when I hear about wars and human interactions involving a lot of violence. I hold a vision of a peaceful world, but these struggles prevent us from making the vision a reality. Conversely, when I hear about amazing acts of kindness, I get tears in my eyes."

SAM: "I feel my will to serve the greater good is typical of an Angel hybrid. From time to time, I feel access to 'intuitive guidance' that may not be that common. I am happiest when I am serving others by building something or watching someone grow."

HELPFUL HINTS FOR ANGEL HYBRIDS

1. Have realistic goals and expectations for yourself and others. You are in the human world now, where none of us are perfect.

2. Forgive yourself for sins of omission (what you have not done) and commission (what you have done)—and the sooner the better. Following the first Hint will help.

3. You may feel an underlying sadness because of your loss of connection to Spirit. Don't worry. Keep on the path. It will be yours again.

4. Trust your inner guidance and intuition, rather than relying upon the opinions of others.

5. Meditate and practice spiritual disciplines regularly to strengthen your connection to Spirit.

ELS

Els are full Creators who are helping the Earth become a conscious planet. El hybrids who have incarnated into human evolution may, or may not, remember their Divine heritage and may need to evolve back to consciousness, just as members of other hybrid races are doing.

Els, a much older race than humans, completed their evolution to become conscious Creators on Sirius, the brightest star system in Earth's night sky. When we complete our evolution in one solar system, Spirit may ask, "Will you help another race develop?"

Els (some but not all) decided to help form the Earth and all the beings on it. Many of them have been on Earth from the very beginning when the Earth was only a ball of gas. Others arrived later.

Although this race may be unfamiliar to you, knowledge of them is recorded in our earliest cultures. In Canaanite texts, from which both Greek and Hebrew Biblical stories derive, the Supreme Deity is called "El", meaning God. He is the final authority in all affairs—human and Divine. One of his titles was Ab Adam meaning "Father of Man" and he was the "Creator of All Things Created". El was described as a kind and merciful elderly deity and, although he did not interfere with daily affairs, he resolved disputes that the other gods brought to him. His home was reputedly in the area of the Tigris and Euphrates, which later became Sumeria.

Humans in many of our ancient cultures treated Els like gods. Two of the chief Egyptian gods, Isis and Osiris, were Els who came from Sirius via Atlantis to found the colony of Egypt. It is said in

Egyptian mythology that Isis and Osiris brought civilisation to humanity by teaching early humans how to domesticate animals and grains.

Els originally did not interbreed with humans, but they have been living as hybrids among humans since late Lemurian and Atlantean times. Many of these hybrids took a vow to remain on the Earth until all beings were enlightened and to assist with this process.

Els, as a race, are strong on the first Ray of Will. In their evolution on Sirius, they used this Will in dedication to the Divine and, as hybrids, they may likewise feel a deep calling to do this.

Els, because they have free will, have had to learn self-restraint and discipline not to use their will for selfish ends and, as hybrids, they usually exhibit this same quality. Els might be seen as stern, uncompromising, and even harsh taskmasters in their supreme dedication to achieving the Creator's goals. El hybrids usually exhibit this same quality, because they are so focused on what they see as the goal and the most efficient way to achieve it.

Great energy, focus, and commitment—qualities of the first Ray of Divine Will—are needed to create a form for any new idea. This is why leaders of new ways of thinking or new types of organizations have a driven quality.

This is true for people, who have characteristics that could be found in an El hybrid—like Mother Theresa, Martin Luther King, and the political leader Nelson Mandela. Although some people learn to work with the first Ray, it may not be their natural strength. El hybrids can teach others to use this quality.

Els hybrids were attracted to the material world and experiences of the senses because their talent is building form. These hybrids learned how to use light and energy to manifest what they wanted in the lower frequencies of form. They also developed a stronger consciousness of self, as well as the quality of love-compassion from being on the Earth.

El hybrids sometimes experience difficulties by becoming attached to sensuality and superficial pleasures, such as possessions and home. Another difficulty is a sense of entitlement ... that they deserve those things. This is an arrogance based on an unconscious, maybe conscious, memory of the great beings they once were. Through inappropriate self-love, they can exaggerate their uniqueness and separateness, forgetting they are now part of the whole of existence. If they are challenged in this way, it is important that they learn humility and exercise severe restraint.

They have strong will and a pioneering spirit for starting new things and, when spiritually developed, they devote their will to helping others. El hybrids are primarily mental, unlike Angel hybrids who have a tendency towards emotion, feeling, and devotion. El hybrids are interested in creating forms, organizations, books, and systems that work. They have clear sight and the ability to intuitively know the truth. They also have a clear sense of purpose, direction, dedication, and consecration—qualities often applauded in warriors. In human terms, there is a sense of the warrior about them.

This does not mean that El hybrids lack love any more than Angel hybrids lack wisdom. El hybrids demonstrate their love primarily through their unswerving commitment to serve the Divine Will; rather like the objective love of a priest than the softer love of Angel hybrids. El hybrids often sacrifice personal relationships to serve Spirit, which is not always the case with Angel hybrids. In yogic terms, an Angel might be attracted more to Bhakti (devotional) yoga, and an El more to Jnana (mental) yoga.

El hybrids may be attracted to Angel hybrids to learn compassion and gentleness, while simultaneously teaching discernment and detachment to the Angel hybrid. This is why Jesus, who taught love, is possibly of Angelic descent, while Gautama Buddha, who taught wisdom, may be of El descent. These paths of love and wisdom are both needed to become a Creator. Often an individual will change paths between love and wisdom for a lifetime—or over many lifetimes—to balance these two qualities.

I have a lot to add about El hybrids as they take a special interest in Elementals—note the "EL" at the beginning of the name. It's not by accident that we are called Elementals and they are called Els. They came to Earth to help humans, but also to help all beings develop consciousness. So Els have been with us from the beginning. And because Elementals live in a lighter etheric frequency than you humans, we have never lost touch with them. Els continue to guide us. Even when Els entered your human world as hybrids, they continued to visit our world to help us. Unlike you, we can always see the essence of a being, so Elementals can spot an El hybrid right off. Actually, we can tell what kind of hybrid every human is, but I don't want to be digressing ... !

To be more exact about how they help, I'd like to point out that Elementals might not have become conscious beings without them. They taught us right from the beginning to develop our minds, to become conscious, and also, of course, to be loyal to Divine Will. Yes ... without them, we certainly might have run amuck.

✎ El Hybrid: ELLIE

"As a child I enjoyed the company of adults. I listened carefully to their conversations and would often take everyone by surprise when I piped in with an observation or comment. I was a kind of know-it-all. I had the feeling on some level I did know it all. Later, I came to realize it was a strong and powerful intuition.

"I suffered because I felt limited in academia and I longed to be 'out of the closet' with the intelligences that I valued most, which were intra- and inter-personal intelligence. These I placed at the center of my research and study for most of my adult life. A colleague of mine, who I enjoyed studying with, turned to me exasperated one day and said, 'You think too much.' I couldn't make sense of that. How could one think TOO MUCH? I have been told that I am like a witch or that I am frightening to men. Recently a man I was interested in told me, 'You scare me … too much knowledge.'

"I have been fiercely focused all my life. This has translated into devoted adherence to spiritual/meditative practice, dream work, study of many approaches to knowledge, i.e., Shamanism, Astrology, Geomancy, Anthroposophical Art therapy, and Biography work. I have a very broad range of interests and I certainly enjoy most of what I pursue. I find it almost unbearable to do something that is not directly connected to learning, growing, or serving in some way. I don't travel just for fun. It is always related to taking a course, giving a course, or pursuing some important research.

"This was difficult in my marriage because I would not attend events or go out if I felt it was not somehow connecting more deeply to my work, or my learning, or the relationships I had made a commitment to. I could not sit and have superficial, social chitchat.

"I have always felt driven; felt that every moment in my life was precious and I worked very hard at everything I have done, always giving one hundred and ten percent. I work when I am awake and I work when I am asleep.

"Spiritually, I am very eclectic. As a teenager, I wore a gold cross, a gold Star of David and a little Buddha simultaneously around my neck. I took this natural ability to create sacred ritual space into my adult life into creating ceremonies that I have conducted over decades for weddings, births, deaths, coming of age, etc. I equally respect all religious paths and spiritual practices.

"During the meditation at the Tanis workshop on Hybrids, I remembered arriving on the planet, having made a vow to stay—no matter how long it took—to help with the development of the Earth. There was no turning back. I came as a helper to the helpers … a servant of many different initiatives. That is the role I've played in this life: making it possible for certain work by certain teachers to take place.

El Hybrid: BARBARA

"I tend to be observant and clear thinking. I have noticed that others let emotions get in the way of their thinking and decision-making. Of course, I have emotional moments, but not on such an every-day-every-issue basis. I am more mentally centered than many and tend to see things from the perspective of logical thinking and planning. I tend to be very organized when I want to accomplish something. Some people think I am too serious and not much fun to work with. For example, I have friends who say they will only work with me if we can have fun.

"I have a tendency to be bossy. I have had to bring this part of my nature under control. But basically, I never saw a situation I didn't think needed to be changed—and that I could change it—and that I know what is best. This can be very annoying to other people, so I have lightened up on this aspect of my outlook on life.

"I have always had a tendency to over-extend. I try to do too much; or as my mother always said about me: 'You burn the candle at both ends'. I'm sure I exhausted her. But I know I exhaust everyone I stay with, so I have had to be aware that I can be 'too much' or 'too energetic' for other people.

"I am a good listener and when others have problems, I am frequently detached enough to see a good solution. I have leadership skills that I can count on if it is appropriate. I have increasingly let others take the reigns, as I have less and less energy these days to solve so many problems. I am intuitive and often see the direction things are going or will go. My gifts are compassionate and clever leadership for vanguard projects that bring useful change and the ability to develop new ways of doing things. I have been a bit of a pioneer in the educational field and in the area of bringing about change."

✎ El Hybrid: PETRA

"Mentally, I am creative, always looking for a solution 'outside the box', and rarely quitting until the goal—whatever it might be, for myself or others—is accomplished. Perhaps the most challenging difficulty I face, for me and those in my life, has been that I always feel I know the best way to do things, the best path for others to take, etc. It has been quite a challenge to learn detachment.

"I am good at creating structure. In this lifetime, I have put that need/ability to good use, both for myself and for others. I had a very successful career as an Incident Commander in Search and Rescue in New Mexico and Colorado. I was in charge of creating the form/structure within which to find missing aircraft, lost hikers and hunters, and provide classes so the general public could help themselves in the wilderness. In my largest search, I had over four hundred people under my command. I also helped run an environmental non-profit for over ten years, plus I raised five children and organized their lives, or should I say, tried to!

"The greatest lesson I have learned in this life as an El hybrid is that it is an amazing gift to have a connection with all beings on this planet, whether they are Elementals, animals, plants, rocks, or humans. After learning about Els, I now understand why I have a need to oversee the world."

HELPFUL HINTS FOR EL HYBRIDS

1. You have a tendency to think that you know better than others what they should do. You might be right, but it is an irritating habit. Find other ways to reframe your opinions and give up attachment to them.

2. The above point might lead to arrogance; another irritating habit. Either you develop humility or the Universe will help you learn it.

3. You are a natural leader and, if this is your destiny, you will be chosen to do this. Serve others with compassion as you serve the Divine.

4. Forgive yourself for not being perfect. You've come a long way, so be tolerant of yourself and others.

5. You are not only on Earth to work, but also to enjoy life on this beautiful planet. Lighten up and play more.

HORUS

There are other Star Beings, besides the Els, who were full Creators in their own star system and who came to Earth to help with the evolution of life forms here. One of these is Garuda, a gigantic eagle-like deity worshipped in Buddhism and Hinduism throughout China, Thailand, and India. One of the earliest references to this deity is found in the ancient Vedas, where this mighty bird by the name of Śyena is said to have brought the nectar of immortality to Earth from Heaven. Considered to be an intelligent, fierce warrior, it is called Raven among the First Nations people of the Pacific Northwest Coast and is said to be the Creator of the world, as well as a trickster. The Cowichan, a coastal indigenous people of British Columbia, believed these beings could take human form and even intermarry into human families.

The American Southwest, Great Lakes, and Great Plain indigenous cultures refer to these beings as Thunderbirds, and the Lakota name for them means "sacred". We might think Thunderbirds are creatures only of our imagination, but many myths, as we have come to know, are based on reality. Even today, farmers throughout central parts of North America have reported seeing Thunderbirds —gigantic birds that emerge, as if out of the Void, prior to violent thunderstorms. They can appear at that time because of the change in electrical polarities between the dimensions where they exist and our third dimension. Although equally intelligent and fierce, Thunderbirds may be a degenerated version of the creatures known as Garuda, Raven, and Horus.

In Egyptian mythology, this same being is referred to as Heru, which means "the distant one", and it is depicted with a head of a falcon. Heru, or Horus, as he is known to the Greeks and more commonly to us, is the child of Isis and Osiris, both of whom are always seen in human form. Horus is a Christ-like figure who fought and won a war with Set, the Egyptian god of the Underworld.

All these myths point to an intelligent bird-like being who has always been involved in human evolution. Supporting evidence has been found in ancient Egyptian records. The Egyptian High Priest Manetho (Ma-n-Thoth), also called "Master of the Secrets", living in the third-century BCE, had access to the library of Alexandria. He wrote a three-volume history of Egypt, the *Aegyptiaca*, in which he reported that the gods Osiris, Horus, and Thoth (among others) reigned from 33,894 to 23,642 BCE. Following this period, the Shemsu Hor, called "Followers of Horus", reigned for another 13,400 years. They are hybrids of humans and sacred bird-like beings.

The royal cannon papyrus displayed at the Museum of Egyptology of Turin, which dates back to Ramses II, presents a list of all the pharaohs who reigned in Egypt. This list includes, not only the historical pharaohs, but also the "divine pharaohs who came from elsewhere" who reigned for 13,420 years before the first dynasty of Menes—the same Followers of Horus hybrids described in Manetho's history of Egypt.

Is there any archeological evidence to substantiate the existence of a pre-diluvian race? Archaeologist Walter B. Emery, author of the book *Archaic Egypt*, found the remains of people living in a pre-dynastic time. Professor Emery identified these people with the Followers of Horus and determined that they filled an important priestly role. Their skulls are larger than present day humans skulls and are dolichocephalic, meaning the cranium, as seen from above, is oval and is about twenty-five percent longer than it is wide. Not only are these skulls larger than average but also the skeletons are broader and heavier.

Such enlarged skulls have been found in Peru among three pre-Inca dolichocephalic races: the Chinchas, Aymara, and Huancas. Some skulls are completely natural, while others have been bandaged to take the oval shape. The oldest pre-Inca city in Peru, Tiahuanaco, dates from the same time as pre-dynastic Egypt, and enlarged skulls from this period can be seen in the Tiahuanaco Museum.

In addition, about 700 of these skulls have been found in the Hypogea of Hal Saflieni and the tombs of the megalithic temples of Taxien and Ggantja in Malta. Dr. Anton Mifsud and Dr. Charles Savona Ventura analyzed the skulls and found three different groups, some of completely natural origin, and others that had been bandaged much like the later Peruvian skulls. This race, as in Egypt, seems to have been devoted to the priesthood and teaching, and kept itself somewhat isolated.

These skulls are no longer on view. Humans are uncomfortable having to rethink their theory of evolution based on findings that do not tally with us evolving from an ape-like creature.

I am not saying these skulls are specifically of the Horus being, yet they are definitely from an older race than Earth's current races and I believe they provide an archeological link to a Star race (or races).

Horus is associated with Isis and Osiris, who came from Sirius originally, but with his falcon head, he is obviously of a different lineage, with clues to his origin found in Sumerian mythology. In Sumeria, the chief god Enlil was the god of breath, wind, loft, and breadth—qualities we associate with birds—and the god Enlil was associated with the star Arcturus.

Dr. Jim Hurtak, in *The Keys of Enoch*, also states that these Horus beings come from Arcturus, and their role is to create evolved life forms in our galaxy by way of genetic manipulation in accordance with the Divine Plan.

Horus beings are involved in the evolution of birds on Earth and are helping them to develop more love and compassion. Birds evolved from cold-blooded dinosaurs, but birds now have become warm-blooded, illustrating that love and affection is growing in them. Many gifts of birds are also gifts of these Horus beings and, therefore, of hybrids with this lineage.

Horus hybrids have a gift of far and clear sight, are able to see the future and the past, and to exist simultaneously in the present, past, and future. Because of their clear sight, Horus hybrids assist beings in other evolutions to discover their essence by reflecting back to them—as a mirror does—who they are. Horus hybrids prefer to be alone, although they entered human evolution to experience being part of a group, being dependent, and joining with others. Horus hybrids usually have a slight body that is nevertheless strong for its weight.

They can see the history of our planet and its entire species, and they save this memory to share with other sentient life forms. The gift of these hybrids, as air beings who live close to the ethers, is to telepathically pick up what is going to happen next and subtle nuances from others. Because they are so sensitive, Horus hybrids can feel rejected easily and yet they have an impatient nature that can quickly become annoyed at others.

The great Horus beings live in much higher dimensions than humans and their hybrids will come into their strength and be appreciated for their gifts even more as we evolve and move to those higher realms. They are committed to serving the Divine and look for ways to do this.

The difficulties they face, as we see in the myths of many cultures, is that if provoked, they can speak or act violently like a warrior to defend themselves and their boundaries.

Horus hybrids might at first appear cool and detached because of their more introverted nature. They are likely to be athletic and love the outdoors and sports. Although they may be married, they often lead quite separate lives and have different interests from their spouses.

*H*orus beings are well-known to Elementals as they live in our dimension, which is a lighter one than you humans live in. It's a bit of a mixed review on them from my standpoint. Smart, yes; committed to Spirit, yes; can travel in many dimensions and show others how to do this, yes. However, just try to get their attention ... there's the difficulty. They are so singularly focused on what they are doing that they tend to get impatient when weaker folks (like Elementals) need help.

Now to be fair, I'm talking only about the ones that are in our dimension. I've heard the ones in higher dimensions have remarkable patience and have been on Earth from the start, working on genetic engineering to improve species. Oh, and another thing: They are committed to bird evolution. They are warriors for the good in higher dimensions as well. Just down here where I am, they have a tendency to be a bit uppity and think themselves a bit better than others.

I can hear my co-author thinking I'm being too hard on them. Well, maybe. I better have some tea to smooth me nerves.

✦ Horus Hybrid: RACHEL

I have a good friend who is a hawk hybrid, and she lives like a hermit. Rachel finds it extremely difficult to be in groups of people or crowds as they are too disturbing for her. She also suffers from skin problems which can sometimes represent a boundary issue with others. She is physically strong, despite a slight build, and seriously studied ballet until adulthood. Rachel does not necessarily agree with all my perceptions of Horus hybrids, or of her for that matter. For this very reason, it is important that she speak for herself.

"I am comfortable by myself and have a small number of close friends, rather than being part of a gang. In meetings, if I think of something relevant that hasn't been said, I will say it. I draw back from emotional intensity and persuasive speech to consider the reverberations within myself and consequences of a plan.

"I am surprised I perceive others differently, sometimes drastically, than my partner. The next task is to examine these differences of perception. Are they the result of different viewpoints, personal histories? Compared to most people, I have more patience in dealing with the irksome—boring, repetitive, self-centered, and slow people. I don't mind waiting. Some things take time. If people get annoyed at my slowness, they would be amazed at my brother. Generally, I don't have a short temper but, with repeated provocation, I react quickly and forcefully and sometimes surprise myself. Two years ago, I hit a nurse who was treating me like a two-year-old child.

"To me, linear time has always co-existed with all time, simultaneously present. Being consciously aware of this is another matter. It comes and goes. The same with space —neither are rigid. I was raised with the ideal of looking beyond oneself. This has outward aspects, obvious to the five senses, and an inner aspect of looking into the shell, honoring the intuitive and (seemingly) random guides."

➹ Horus Hybrid: HANNA

"Physically, I squeak. I have two separate holes where my upper jaw, behind my front teeth, did not come together all the way. I can pull air down through my nostrils into my mouth, which results in a high-pitched chirp that sounds like a bird. I have met one other person who has this ability.

"I have always had a slender build and was a good athlete (varsity level in many sports); but I am clumsy. Sexually, I have never been interested. Sometimes I want to be touched, but I'm afraid at the same time.

"Emotionally, I've been a loner all my life. I was a shy child and very private. Hated being in situations where I had to make conversation. Never felt really part of any group, but had friends in all the groups. Being alone is wonderful! I've always enjoyed being by myself more than being with others. Never needed a group to feel worthy but, when I was around other people, I felt I needed their praise to feel worthy in their eyes—and then mine. In this lifetime, I am consciously trying to be with people and share my spirit.

"Expressing my thoughts is difficult. It doesn't always come out the way I want. It is hard to express, find the right words, and remember things on the spot. Also, keeping focused on a conversation with someone for a long time is really hard. My mind wants to think about something else. I get frustrated because I know I know ... but I can't articulate what I want to say. Finally, at this stage of my life, I say, "Oh, well. It will come to me sometime, or not!" No big deal any more.

"For the first half of my life, I was very sensitive to how

others perceived me, mentally and physically. Feelings of rejection came easily, therefore, I could not feel part of a group. I get impatient and can be annoyed by people who keep bringing up their life story and are stuck there. 'Get over it and move on' is what I want to say. Since I like being alone, it is hard to take the time to work at being part of a group. Another difficulty is learning authentic compassion, royal giving, connecting with others, and serving them. If I concentrate, I can feel how others are feeling and put myself in their place, so I know it is possible.

"My gift is that I am good with craft-making and with color and tactile awareness. I love playing the Native American Flute, connecting with the flow of the air and vibrations, and how I can sound like a bird. Hearing the flute takes people to another level of listening, feeling, consciousness, and helps them soar. I am loyal and committed to God, the Divine Spirit, and I trust God. I can now share that with other people and be myself.

"I knew that God, the Divine Spirit, would always take care of me, no matter what I had to face in this lifetime. I never knew where that came from; I just graciously accepted it. It is sad to me that other people don't have that understanding in their lives. The greatest lesson I have learned is that God is in all things and that my love, trust, and compassion need to extend to all living things. To love God is wonderful, but to love all creatures and things created by God is true love."

HELPFUL HINTS FOR
HORUS HYBRIDS

1. Let go of perfectionist tendencies that make you impatient with yourself and others.

2. Realize you are a human. You have entered this evolution so you are one of us. This has good and bad points: Accept them.

3. You have remarkable talents that are often unappreciated at this stage in human evolution. Love the individuals who see and accept you and be patient with the others. Your time will come.

4. Love is what you are here to learn. Celebrate all the people and ways that you have learned it.

5. Practice telepathically communicating your ideas and thoughts to others when you have difficulty expressing verbally.

PAN

Pan beings came originally from the stars, where they were full Creators. They are committed to look after the Elementals on Earth. In Greek mythology, Pan was a son of the Sun god Cronos, who later became the father of Zeus, one of the earliest Olympians. Pan gave hunting dogs to Artemis and taught Apollo the gift of prophecy, which indicates that he was older than the Olympian gods.

Pan's worship was well established in Thrace, the larger part of which is modern-day Bulgaria, and further back with the Cimmerian civilization. These two cultures have a common Indo-European derivation.

In even earlier stories from the middle Bronze Age, the Sea-Goat was connected to the constellation Capricorn and was depicted as a goat with a fish tail. This relationship could indicate why Pan is often represented as having goat feet and horns on a human torso. In Babylon, Capricorn was associated with their god Ea, the god of the water—another myth connecting Pan beings with the constellation Capricorn.

Pan enters recorded history when Midas, the king of Phrygia between 718 and 709 BCE and called Mitta-a by contemporary Assyrians, prefers Pan's rustic flute playing to that of Apollo. It is likely the worship of Pan extended originally throughout Ethiopia, Libya, Arabia, and perhaps even India.

In later times, Pan worship was linked to the Greek god Dionysus, the son of Zeus who was raised by Nymphs in the wilderness. The cult of Dionysus was closely associated with trees, specifically the fig tree, which may refer to Dionysus being at home in the woods.

This reference might also mean Dionysus is connected to the World Tree, the Tree of Life, and kundalini energy. Dionysus is a dying god who helps his followers undergo a spiritual death and resurrection. This is a gift of Pan and Pan hybrids as well.

The companions of both Pan and Dionysus were Satyrs or little Pans who looked like and behaved like Pan. Many of Dionysus's talents were subsumed from Pan. When cultures change, the new culture replaces older gods with newer ones who fit what is valued in the new culture.

For example, ancient images of Dionysus depict him as a mature, bearded man, not unlike Pan. Later, the Greeks (lovers of physical beauty) replaced the hairy, chubby goat-like Pan creature with a physically attractive, often naked, robust young man—the current image of Dionysus..

In both Hebrew and Arab folklore, there are references of sacrificing to shaggy devils of the mountain; the English translation of these "hairy ones" became Satyrs in the *King James Bible*. When Christianity replaced former nature and pagan religions, the word Satyr became Satan, and Pan and his followers were referred to as evil.

Let's look at the gifts of Pan and Dionysus, as these are the ones who point the way for Pan hybrids within human evolution.

Pan and Dionysus are uninhibited sexually and attracted to both male and female lovers. Although Pan hybrids may not feel this desire physically, they feel love in their hearts for both men and women to a depth that other human hybrids seldom experience. Pan hybrids may seek intimate, if not sexual, relationships with both genders.

Both Pan and Dionysus love music and wine, and drank, danced, and had excessive sex to achieve ecstasy. This was not only for physical reasons, but also to achieve a communion with Spirit, a great desire of Pan hybrids. This completely unrestrained way of worshiping is contrary to that found in Judaic and Christian worship. Pan hybrids are not drawn to traditional religions and are often willing to live outside the boundaries of what is considered the cultural norm.

Physically, Pan and his companions are hairy with the hindquarters, legs, and horns of a goat. He has a round belly and, in older depictions, is bearded with an ivy wreath in his hair. In Greek mythology, Pan was the god of shepherds and flocks. Pan hybrids prefer to live in wild, remote natural settings and woodlands. They have a gift of fertility, sexuality, and music. When I think of famous people who suggest characteristics of a Pan hybrid, the highly promiscuous and charismatic ballet dancer Rudolf Nureyev comes to mind.

One of my Pan hybrid friends actually has knobs in his scull where horns would be and his physique is very Pan-like. He is generous-hearted and women love him, which Pan hybrids have in common. He plays a wind instrument and is involved in healing techniques that employ mind-altering plants.

Pan and his Satyr followers are known to be attracted to Nymphs. According to Greek mythology, Nymphs animate nature and come in five categories: Celestial, Water, Land, Plant, and Underworld. They dwell in mountains, forests, by springs and rivers, and do not die of old age or illness, yet they are not immortal. Nymphs love to dance and sing and enjoy sex. Obviously, this is a description of Elementals. Pan hybrids are attracted to elemental women and vice versa!

Other cultures have Pan-like beings as well. Kokopeli, in the American Southwest, is a similar kind of wild creature who played the flute like Pan. When Kokopeli entered towns, the women and children would follow him into the wild, leaving behind their husbands and civilization. Kokopeli had sexual gifts to help women conceive, and he was more fun to play with, so the local men were often jealous. The townsmen represent the jealousy that can arise in men, bound to reason, who cannot let themselves be intimate with their children or their wives—or even themselves.

Kokopeli and Pan use their kundalini energy for creativity, sexuality, pleasure, and spiritual transformation. The gift of a Pan hybrid is to help men, children, and women release their sexual inhibitions, as well as their joy.

However, their good hearts and healing qualities are often misunderstood and their wounding occurs when others, either jealous or afraid of such gifts, reject them.

Pan hybrids have a gift with the fire of de-manifestation. Like Goblin hybrids, Pan hybrids see what needs to be released and de-manifested in an individual, organization, or garden, and they excel at removing the dead wood to bring back health and vitality. Not all people want to be around this quality fulltime, which means although attracted to them, they do not want to be around Pan hybrids. This is the paradox that Pan hybrids must learn to accept.

Pan hybrids have more difficulty in manifesting than de-manifesting, as they manifest by removing what does not work or fit, so what is left then returns to health. They are often isolated in our culture, which does not value this great and distinctive gift as the Pan hybrid's greatest contribution.

Pan loves Elementals and is always helping them with their evolution. They regard Pan as one of their main teachers because he is associated with wild places and woodlands.

*T*hat "other writer" was keen to write this, but it is my turn. Share and share alike. Anyway, she's bound to agree with what I'm saying.

We Elementals love the Great God Pan and he is, still, and will always be our main god as he is a Nature god. We also love his companions, the Satyrs, for the same reason. Many of them work with us even today in our realm. We are familiar with the Christ and love him, too, but for us Elementals, it's Pan who understands us and is like us. We relate to him better.

Tanis did not mention that Pan is a Christ figure. Jesus took the Pan and Dionysus story of the god who dies and is reborn and absconded with it, which is fine, as long as Christians admit that Elementals can evolve and ascend as well as they can. Pan is an enlightened being and is the Head of Elementals, working with the human Karmic Board to decide which Elementals can enter human evolution as hybrids. Yeah, Pan!

✣ Pan Hybrid: RUFUS

"My mother told me I was born with a mane of downy hair along my spine that disappeared in a few days. As a child, I didn't play much with toys. I was always outdoors and in the woods. My favorite place was at the brook or river near the waterfall at the back of our property. I wasn't allowed at the river because of the danger of falling in, but I wasn't very good at obedience when it interfered with a chance to play! By the time I was ten, my dad said he didn't know what to do with me … I seemed to be living my own nature life.

"I brought joy to the adults in my small community in rural Nova Scotia by listening to their woes with eagerness and always lending a helping hand. I was full of imagination and practical ideas of how to make adult's lives easier. But this innovativeness was usually brushed aside as it was too unconventional. I told my mom that when I grew up, I would rather sweat than work behind a desk.

"By age twenty, I had a spiritual awakening after sailing for twenty-eight days to Hawaii from Vancouver. I became a spiritual healer and came to know that spiritual home was a reality beyond just belief. I knew that society had lost its natural rhythms. After years of traditional and cosmic spiritual study, I started learning native and shamanic Earth spirituality. Trees and plants would sporadically give me messages about people who came to me for help. I also got messages or 'energy niggles' from roots of trees. Eventually, my body became a truth meter. Clients may have their story, but my body would tell me where their emotion was blocked.

"All my life has been about flow and removing blocks. As a child, I frequently would get blocked ditches or mud puddles flowing. Everyone confided in me. Today, in my coaching work, I sometimes refer to myself as a 'story catcher for matters of the heart'. I sense the blockages in my client's stories and coach them to face and shift the emotional blocks holding them back from creating the life they want. I help them see their true nature ... their true self. I hear this feedback repeatedly from my questing and coaching clients and workshop participants."

⌇ Pan Hybrid: WOLFGANG

"In my body, I always have the wish/need to be and move in nature, to feel myself whole. However, I am not so sure-footed and feel I am missing the road adhesion and contact with the earth. Sexuality is a very important part of my life and I express this with my partner. I can feel during sex when something separates us. I am visual and love to look at the beauty of my wife naked. My big wish is to make her happy.

"One of my biggest powers is my capacity for enthusiasm, which influences other people and my environment in a positive way. On the other side, I am a little reserved in what I say because I have great respect for that which is spoken aloud. I believe strongly in justice and quickly try to find the balance in situations that are out of balance. My emotions can be very hot and fiery, but I can cool down fast to normal balanced emotions. It is easy for me to connect myself intuitively. Sometimes people, with whom I have a close relationship, see me as arrogant. I think this is because I have a strong core of inner wisdom, which others find a bit unusual.

"Since childhood I have believed that, because of my feeling of being different from other humans, people couldn't understand me, and I seldom found the key to express myself in the right way. Sometimes those close to me get irritated and explode, and I often don't understand why this happens.

"Although I can feel isolated, people like me most of the time because I have the gift of listening to what others are saying and, on the heart dimension, I am deeply compassionate. People trust me and tell me things they wouldn't tell others. I've been told I should become a priest because of these gifts.

"My capacity to concentrate is my most difficult point because my thoughts tend to fly in different directions. I am both right- and left-handed; this is not so good for brain concentration. This can makes me feel insecure mentally. I have a clear inner image of my personal values, but find it difficult to bring my surroundings on to this same path. I have to struggle to bring my thoughts and intentions together with actual reality.

"Since early childhood, spirituality has been an important part of my life. I already had my secret altar, a place to be near God. I feel the presence of holiness, especially in nature and I always wanted to bring positivity into the world.

"I feel my greatest gift is to be responsible for Mother Earth. I am thankful for what I have learned about my hybrid nature. I understand better now how I can integrate my authentic self in the world. In my friendship with other hybrids, I understand more aspects about their behavior and why they act in specific ways. This has helped me to expand my compassion."

HELPFUL HINTS FOR PAN HYBRIDS

1. Human males will often feel threatened by you because of your sexual power and the fact that so many women are attracted to you. Just be true to yourself.

2. Human females will either a) completely trust you, so be careful not to betray this trust, or b) being nervous about their own sexuality and instincts, will not trust yours either. Be gentle to both.

3. Instincts are undervalued in our present-day advanced civilization, so your talents are also undervalued. There will always be those who see you. Be grateful for them.

4. Find ways to use your gifts of de-manifestation.

5. Make sure that you are in nature daily. This is food to you and will keep you happy and healthy.

DRAGON

R eferences to Dragons go far back in human history. The star Alpha Draconis, also called Thuban, the Arabic word for "snake", is in the constellation of Draco, which was the Northern Pole star from 3942 until 1793 BCE.

The Dragon has great power—the power of magic. And they know how to work with all four elements. A Dragon can fly (air); it can swim in and under the water (water); it can live on the land in caves (earth); and it breathes and shoots flames (fire).

Let us examine many mythologies around the world to better understand the qualities of dragons and their hybrids.

European and Oriental depictions of Dragons both speak of them as hatching from eggs, resembling a serpent, and having either feathers or scales on their body. European Dragons have wings whereas Oriental ones usually do not.

Dragons, in Chinese and Oriental mythology, are generally benevolent, wise, revered, and represent primal forces of Nature and the Universe. European Dragons, on the other hand, are usually seen as malevolent. Why the different interpretation? In Greek mythology, Dragons were one of the species of great Titans that the Olympian gods fought and replaced. Often in myth former gods are vilified by later ones. We see this also in Christianity, where dragons became identified with evil. Archangel Michael and St. George were often portrayed slaying Dragons, which were associated with sexuality and early pagan beliefs.

In Mesoamerica, the Dragon is found as the feathered serpent Quetzalcoatl. The worship of Quetzalcoatl began in the first century

BCE and continued until Cortez's arrival in America in the early sixteenth century. Quetzalcoatl is a Christ-like figure whose mother was said to be either a virgin to whom the god Onteol appeared in a dream, or the Creator Mother God, Coatlicue, who formed all the stars of the Milky Way.

Quetzalcoatl, as in Chinese mythology, was benevolent. He was credited in Mesoamerica with going to the underworld to create humanity for our current fifth-world cycle of evolution. He created humans from the bones of the previous races and by using his own blood. He brought civilization to humanity through the invention of books and the calendar, taught us to grow corn, and sometimes, was a symbol of death and resurrection.

Dragons are real beings that exist in a higher frequency than us, which is why few of us have seen them. The Great Cosmic Dragon is the head of the Dragons, as Pan is the god of Elementals, and Christ is the spiritual head of humanity. This Cosmic Dragon is a being of great wisdom that is coming closer to us to watch and assist with the birth of the Earth, and to welcome our planet into the community of conscious planets. The symbol of this process is found in the Chinese tradition and depicted as a Dragon encircling the Cosmic Egg.

Currently, the Cosmic Dragon is brooding the Earth, and the shell—the "ring-pass-not" that surrounds Earth—is starting to crack. This Cosmic Dragon has the responsibility to open the ring-pass-not that protects inhabitants on other planets in our and other solar systems from humans, and us from them.

The Cosmic Dragon works with the kundalini energy of the Earth, which is the electromagnetic leylines, also known as Dragon lines, to catalyze a rise in consciousness of the Earth. Some of you may dream or have visions about Dragons as the Cosmic Dragon and his kin come closer to Earth and, when your frequency rises, you will be able to see them.

The Cosmic Dragon is bringing new cosmic energies into our solar system. It gathers the substances from the etheric, which are needed in the new age that we are entering. This divine creature activates our higher chakras so we are able to enter a new state in our evolution. It works with the Karmic Board to judge exactly when our pineal gland needs to be opened to awaken our dormant DNA. In this way, humanity will be readied to access the cosmic information that has not been available to it until now.

Dragons, although fiercely independent, are very aware and accepting of a hierarchical system under which they operate, with the Cosmic Dragon at the top. Beneath him are Dragons with many different talents, each one excelling on a certain Ray of Power. These Rays are like the gemstones that Dragons are portrayed as coveting in our myths because Dragons and Dragon hybrids, who have entered human evolution, attempt to learn to use all Rays of Energy. Through using the power of all Rays, Dragon hybrids can become either black magicians or, if used for spiritual purposes, enlightened masters.

Dragons are often called upon to judge other races as their talents are will and wisdom. However, their weakness, and that of Dragon hybrids, is that they have not acquired love to the same extent as the other two qualities needed to become a full Creator. Dragons and Dragon hybrids have come to Earth to develop this quality because, without love and compassion, Dragons will be unable to vivify their decisions to make them living—not static—laws.

Dragons and Dragon hybrids have a gift for speaking with the fire of pure truth, which allows them to show humanity the path to wisdom. Like Dragons, hybrids are typically long-lived and very intelligent. Both dragons and dragon hybrids are good at using their kundalini (fire) energy in sexual, creative, healing, and spiritual ways and they are often drawn to the arcane arts and metaphysics.

The best and worst of their Dragon hybrid qualities come out in relationships with partners or children. They are loyal and protective and will do anything for those they love. At the same time, they may have to overcome detachment, coolness, even disdain, when their loved ones turn out to not be as strong or competent as they are. Dragon hybrids must learn to rise above needing to make others into what the hybrid thinks they should be.

Weaknesses of Dragon hybrids, like those of Dragons, are pride and feelings of superiority. This can lead to arrogance, even if they do not express this in words. They have an over-sensitive ego and are easily offended if their talents are not recognized. It is not easy for Dragon hybrids when forced by Spirit to learn humility. They might also have problems with greed and wanting to hoard their possessions. They need to freely share their time, energy, money, and themselves, not only with their own family, but also with all others. In addition, because of their fire energy, they sometimes have trouble giving up smoking.

When I think of people who could be said to exhibit dragon hybrid characteristics, the 20th century occultists and mystics Madame Blavatsky and C. W. Leadbeater come to mind. They are well known in esoteric circles for founding the Theosophical Society, whose members study the western mysteries and ancient knowledge. Both Blavatsky and Leadbeater travelled to the East to study with spiritual masters in the late twentieth century, and many people today credit them with being instrumental in starting the New Age movement. Both Blavatsky and Leadbeater were charismatic, magnetic individuals with clairvoyant powers who drew people who either exalted or condemned them.

Dragons are powerful protectors; even Chinese emperors chose Dragons for their symbol, and Dragons will fiercely protect those in their care. Many children are currently seeing Dragons and feeling drawn to them because they need strong protectors to grow up in the world of today.

I'd like to share a story with you about how the Cosmic Dragon is influencing us presently:

A few years ago, our International Institute for Transformation organized a summer camp for children and their families, and it was especially helpful for children who had spiritual experiences. In one visualization exercise, I asked both adults and children to discover an Elemental who wished to work with them. The adults shared their experiences first, and they had received all manner of Fairies, Brownies, and Elves to work with. When the children shared their experiences, each one of them had received a Dragon. What was especially unusual about this occurrence was that neither I, nor any other person, had made reference to Dragons during the week.

The children's Dragons came in all shapes and sizes. They could speak with the children telepathically and told them what qualities they had, and how they were helping each child. In the circle was an autistic teenager, by the name of Michael, who had not spoken with any of us during the week.

I asked, "Michael, did you receive a Dragon?" He nodded yes. Turning to his mother, Michael asked her to tell us that the dragon was blue, it was protecting him, and he could ride it.

I love to speak about Dragons. Little (we're talking physical stature) people, like us Elementals, give them mixed reviews. On one hand, nothing is more majestic than a Dragon or a mature well-developed Dragon hybrid. Royal, beautiful, powerful. However, not very tolerant of what they regard as their lessors. We have had a few very wise and patient Dragons in our realm who taught us to use the power of fire in manifestation and we're thankful to them.

Still, a lot of Dragons would regard working with us as beneath them. Let's just say that in terms of talents, we are at the opposite of the scale (get it? Dragons... scales... Gawd, with humans you have to spell out everything!). Elementals like to play; Dragons are serious. Elementals like to make fun of others; Dragons don't like to be made fun of—no humor that I can see. What they do respect though, is a game of wits, and I've won a few points using my wits with a Dragon or two, which as you can imagine is no easy task.

➤ Dragon Hybrid: LYNDA

"My awareness of being a Dragon hybrid has provided a depth and a meaning to my life unlike any other insight I have had in this lifetime. In reflecting on my Dragon self, I was gifted with the following images and memories"

"Flying, wide wing span, swimming with ease, awkward on land; immense, watching-over, calm presence, wise, protective guardian, fierce/fiery only as required to protect; rocks, rocky landscape, friendly, solo—no mate; guardian of the Earth; heartfelt connection/caring for the human race; sent to protect and support.

"I come from a far away place—misty, formless spirit world. Shapeless yet the same essence as when in solid form; just a speck, waiting to come forward into shape and form; a speck with purpose, with encoding; definition and my mission all encoded; a speck floating in a sea of specks, floating on a wave of energy—a comfortable eternal rocking. From there I came and to there I shall return; similar cells comfortably clustered together like the colors of the rainbow; created and lovingly held by a pulsing eternal source Energy/ Intelligence/Creator.

"Floating in space, the eternal rocking, timeless, effortless, the heart of the continuum, akin to the deepest of meditations, sweetness, joy, balance, grace, effortless flow. This lasted a long time until I heard the call. Slowly awakening—ready to be birthed, no expectations, simple readiness. Dragon wings emerge; I flap them dry. I hover above the egg—cracked and empty. A gentle whisper guides me to my new location—not Earth; another solar system—larger, expansive, endless; a planet very unlike Earth; a planet forming; swirling mists as yet shapeless.

"I breathe fire into the atmosphere quickening the creation. Shapes take form. Mountains, rock formations, water. I stay for millennia, patiently watching over the planet. No beginning, no end. A Dragon suspended in space, rocked in the tide of energy surrounding the planet until one day life emerges. Simple cells, evolving into larger more complex life forms. Still there—breathing life into the planet—content to be and serve my purpose.

"Work is done. I leave. Flying through time and space. Galaxies pass by—where to? My wings spread and I become an emblem in the heavens, a constellation of stars in the shape of a dragon holding the 'field', a part of the All.

"Millennia pass. I am summoned forth again. This time to Earth. China, Egypt, Africa—watching over early civilizations. Earth incarnation as a Dragon in China. Community of Dragons but no mate, per se.

"China was a peaceful place of human growth. Dragons floated over the early civilization holding a 'field' that supported this growth. We were protectors and enablers. The Chinese knew we existed. We lived in harmony connected energetically. We showed ourselves to wise rulers and people connected to spirit. It was a beautiful period of peace and harmony—everything in balance.

"Another existence as a Dragon over Egypt—same role, as civilization developed there. I asked for a new role/variety and I was granted a human incarnation: a woman; ruling, powerful, wise, cool, calm, collected. In Egypt, I incarnated to learn to balance power and wisdom, yin and yang; the challenge of being a woman in power and a wise ruler—strong yet compassionate.

"Did I have Dragon friends/partners? No. Nor did I miss it. The Source was my constant companion, my endless joy, as I watched civilizations come and go, aware of my purpose, no expectations, no deviations, divine purpose in action.

"Was I known to humans? Yes, to those who were connected to the Divine—those who saw beyond the mists. To them I would whisper, messages from the Source. I'd encourage and offer silent support.

"In this present incarnation, I am here to hold the field, to help humans grow as we move towards the shift to higher consciousness; to find opportunities to teach, to influence, to support. My human challenges are to practice humility, yet be in my power; give space to those I love to live their own lives as I love fiercely and am fiercely protective; to be patient with the lack of logic and intelligence in others; and to embrace all humans without judgment. Interestingly, I find it challenging to walk comfortably on the Earth as my Dragon self flies."

HELPFUL HINTS FOR
DRAGON HYBRIDS

1. Practice the following phrases as needed, "I'm sorry." "I apologize for hurting you." "I don't know the answer."

2. Loosen your reigns and all will come to you quicker than if you hold them tight.

3. Don't overreact to what you see as personal slights or criticisms.

4. Of all the hybrids, you have the most power, but service is difficult for you. Dedicate yourself to giving your assistance humbly and freely to all who need you. This is the quickest way to YOUR goal, which is to become a Master of the Universe.

5. Never succumb to the temptation to use your talents for less than honorable ways. It is your greatest temptation and the start of a slippery slope.

CENTAUR

T here are two images of a Centaur in Greek mythology:

1. A horse-like being with four legs and hooves as the lower part of its body; the upper part is a human torso, with two arms, hands, and a human head.
2. Chiron, the most famous centaur in Greek mythology. He has the back legs of a horse while his front legs are human. He usually wears clothes, unlike the depictions of the four-legged Centaurs.

The ancient Greeks thought of the four-legged Centaurs as wild, overly sexual, often intoxicated and uncivilized. Conversely, they said very different things about Chiron. He appears to be the Original Being from the Stars whereas the four-legged Centaurs may be hybrid crosses of Horse and the Star race to which Chiron belongs. Chiron's father was the sun god Cronos, who turned into a horse to have sex with a Sea Nymph. One of his daughters, by another Nymph, was called "truly a mare". This indicates that Chiron established a race of hybrids with a more horse-like appearance and less civilized behaviors.

Centaurs have been associated with Horses throughout history. In Greek myths, the constellation Centaurus was the original home of Chiron. The stars in this constellation are the closest to our own solar system, and it is possible that a race from this constellation came to Earth later than the other Star races. One indication to assess how long a Star race has been on Earth is to examine the myths that arose. Stories about the Centaur are confined to a relatively small geographical area, indicating it has relatively recent origins.

The Greeks said Centaurs lived in Thessaly, Arcadia, and southern Laconia. Chiron was treated as a god in Thessaly. He was especially long-lived and said to be immortal. He also appears to be a younger god than the gods Apollo and Artemis who taught him; again indicating that Centaurs appeared on Earth later than some of the other Star Beings.

The Centaur is also associated by the ancient Greeks as being the constellation Sagittarius—not Centaurus. This contradiction in Chiron's origin is easily explained. Contemporary astronomers know the area of Sagittarius as the Galactic Center and the image of Sagittarius is not wholly the image of a two-legged Centaur like Chiron, but one with wings, a scorpion stinger on its rump, and two heads—one human; the second head, a panther. The Sagittarian image is a composite of many Star races rather than only a Centaur.

I believe the Galactic Center is the origin of our Creator who created the many Star races. The Sumerians, preceding the Greeks by several thousand years, would concur. They called this Sagittarian being "Pailsaq", which means "forefather" or "chief ancestor".

Chiron, renowned by the Greeks as both a prophet and astronomer, pointed his hero Jason towards the Galactic Center in Sagittarius to help guide him in his search for the Golden Fleece. Jason lived prior to the Greek dark ages (1100 BCE), and the Golden Fleece was the Greek equivalent of the Holy Grail. Chiron was guiding Jason on a spiritual quest to find God. It explains how Chiron could have come from Centaurus, not Sagittarius, and how he was pointing Jason towards the home of all Star races—not his specific Centaur race.

Chiron was intelligent, strict, and kind. He taught many famous Greek heroes over hundreds of years. These heroes included

Theseus, Jason, Hercules, and Achilles, all of whom considered him a foster father as well as teacher. Centaur hybrids, like Chiron, put their energy into nurturing others to become heroes rather than be heroes themselves. Their heroism is found in their dedication to others. In addition to tutoring heroes, Chiron is credited with teaching songs, dances, and initiations to young Dionysius. Chiron, like Pan, shared the gift of music.

Although Chiron was much beloved by his students, he was killed by one of them, though in error. Hercules shot poison arrows at a group of four-legged Centaurs he had inadvertently maddened with wine fumes. One of the arrows struck Chiron by mistake. Although Chiron was able to heal others, he was unable to heal himself and was in a great deal of unending pain. Chiron willingly gave up his immortality to Prometheus and was allowed to die. The theme of betrayal, whether by lack of forethought or deliberate, runs deeply in Centaur hybrids. They may be very loyal and dedicated parents and spouses. Yet they can feel betrayed by those closest to them, and often for good reason.

A minor planet, also a comet, in our solar system was named Chiron when astronomers discovered it in 1977 (although images of Chiron have been found going back as far as 1895). Astrologers refer to Chiron as "the wounded healer" and use Chiron's position in an individual's chart to predict that person's deepest wound.

Centaur hybrids, like Chiron, are born teachers. They love to teach and find respect in this field. Centaur hybrids have a gift for healing and Chiron was the foster father and tutor of Asclepius, who became the Father of Medicine. Chiron's great suffering symbolizes the transformative power of illness and affliction. Through physical and psychological pain and suffering, we can transform ourselves and acquire great moral and spiritual strength. The gift of Centaur hybrids is not in healing the emotions in the way Dolphins and

Whales do, but in understanding good physical practices that lead to healing, i.e., keeping a positive attitude, getting sleep, and nurturing a peaceful environment. Centaur hybrids have the knowledge and ability to point someone in the direction of their own healing. They are experienced guides more than hands-on healing practitioners. For example, they would much prefer to write about healing than to spend time giving a massage.

The American writer John Updike wrote a book titled *The Centaur.* Updike is pre-occupied in his writing with themes of sexuality, religion, and death—all preoccupations that would interest a Centaur hybrid. Centaur hybrids would most likely be large-boned. Although they may look strong, they may have problems with joints, or difficulty with their feet not being totally grounded.

Centaur hybrids are very sexual, but their sexuality is often wounded. They may have been victims of adultery or committed adultery themselves. Wanting to nurture and teach the young is a theme of Centaur hybrids, although their children (or people they think of as child-like) often see them as too old-fashioned or strict. They can be very deep thinkers, pondering on secrets of the universe, while remaining realistic and practical in their desire to make society a better place, and simultaneously remain quite traditional in their personal lives at home with family. This dichotomy of old and new might be confusing for them.

A Centaur female, called a Centauress, has the same qualities as the male. They feel things deeply. In Greek myth, the Centauress Hylonome commited suicide when her lover was killed. Like the males, they can be overtaken by passion and do drastic things in their attempt to see themselves. Yet, at the same time, they want people to see them as fair and reasonable.

E *lementals are very fond of Centaur hybrids who are a lot more*
fun than the original Centaurs ever were. Because Centaurs
are a recent Star race on this planet, they can be overly eager to
teach and have others conform to their expectations. Elementals
like to have fun and play with Centaur hybrids and are not always
as conforming as these hybrids would wish. It is good for Centaur
hybrids to lighten up and play more—don't you think?

Centaur hybrids feel a great responsibility to prove themselves.
They're worried that, if they don't do a good job, they'll never get
another opportunity to help a developing race. Anyway, they are
doing a good job! They'd do an even better job, if they didn't push
or try so hard. We know where their fear comes from, as Elementals
can see it, but (hope you are listening, Centaur hybrids) it's time to
enjoy us and this planet more. When you clamp down on yourselves
too hard and go all moralizing, you have a tendency to be too dour
—or to go the other extreme and run amuck. If you give yourselves
more rope, it will help you to stay in healthy territory.

You may think it strange that a member of a younger race than
you is lecturing you. I find it strange meself. I'm giving you good
advice though. You have so much knowledge and wisdom and are a
lot closer to us than a lot of the other Star races—being as you have
an amoral streak like Pan hybrids. You just need to be yourselves
and we will love you even better. I know that to be loved is what you
are really after.

❧ Centaur Hybrid: JOHN

"I believe all humans have a Buddhist nature and
my responsibility is to seek out that Truth. It is my
responsibility to find deeper spiritual truth through
meditation, good works, and helping my fellow man and

community where I can. I have a deep interest in who Jesus really was and have spent years researching and exploring that field.

"I am realistic and practical in wanting to make society a better place. Factual knowledge will not get me where I want go. Inner understanding and action is necessary to get there. I have volunteered in many projects to help the environment. I regularly cleaned the creeks and rivers in the Oakville area with other volunteers. I have taken students to Carrera National Park in Costa Rica to do rainforest restoration work. I took a group of students to Ho Chi Minh City to work in an orphanage.

"Wanting to nurture and teach the young has been a lifelong purpose. I can't think of anything that would have given me greater satisfaction than this line of work. I believe I was born to be a teacher. It is more than knowing the facts of geography, world issues, and environmental studies; it's an innate ability to present information and work with teenagers that is life enhancing and a joy. I have found respect in this work, culminating in winning 'Teacher of the Year' in my city and the Prime Minister of Canada's 'Award for Teaching Excellence'. The kids I worked well with were the 'sweathogs', the socially isolated kids who could spend lunch and after school in my classroom as a safe place.

"I am very sexual by nature. I was wounded during my teen years when being an awkward, rural male lent itself to many rejections. I still don't like answering the phone as it was usually bad news. I had a variety of relationships in the past, in all likelihood seeking the love I craved during adolescent years. I think this is true for many males who weren't the most popular during high school years.

"I love being creative. I play and write music, I'm involved in photography and write poetry. My writings deal with the human condition in all its amazing variety. My style is not a traditional form, but is open and creative in structure.

"I practice a variety of healing techniques including Reiki, Vitaflex (acupressure), Thai, and Swedish massage. In this way, I am looking at physical practices that lead to healing. In my own case, cancer and a broken neck were, in part, made well by remaining positive and facing difficulties with a sense of humor.

"In the past, I had a control issue with temper. This I inherited from my father. Over the years, this has become less of a problem. I'm working at staying in neutral when my temper starts rising.

"I love being surrounded by nature. I grew up in the country on a small hobby farm. Since then, I have lived beside Lake Ontario, on the Niagara Escarpment, on a three-acre property surrounded by horses and fruit trees and at present, close to the Pacific Ocean and majestic mountains.

"I have learned to remain open-minded. Years of travel, a seven-year experience in Hong Kong, and experiences during past life regression have shown me that, what the human mind thinks is real, may be an illusion. As for my Centaur reality from a physical perspective, hmmm ... I'm quite hairy."

HELPFUL HINTS FOR
CENTAUR HYBRIDS

1. You prefer the role of expert to any other role and must learn humility when others outshine you.
2. You have a tendency to see any sign of disagreement with your views as a personal attack. It seldom is, so remember to stay in neutral when your temper starts rising.
3. As Leprechaun Lloyd said, love is what you really want. You will receive this through the help you give others from your generous heart.
4. In many areas, you are a fount of knowledge. Others appreciate this the more they get to know you. We encourage you to write, as you do it well, and you will earn respect, which is very important to you.
5. You are a natural big brother/sister/mentor for young people. Seek ways to serve in this way.

BEE

This next hybrid will likely come as a surprise to many. Bees, you may say, are only insects and, therefore, at the bottom of the evolutionary ladder, while humans are at the top. Wrong! Just as humans may have judgements about birds, and doubt how Horus could be an advanced soul, we need to release lessening assumptions about Bees.

The Mayans believed that the Bee came from the planet Venus, which they referred to as the "Second Sun". Modern Bees are minor versions of a highly intelligent race that is native to Venus and are one of the earlier attempts to integrate Venusian life on Earth. Members of the Bee race came to Earth at the end of one of our earlier evolutionary cycles and their purpose was to hold the Earth from sinking into darkness. More is written about this in my book *Decoding Your Destiny*.

Many qualities of the Bee hybrid are reflected in the Greek myth of Cupid, the child of Venus, the goddess of love (another reference to Venus as in the Mayan myth). Cupid, also known as Eros (love) in Roman myth, carries two kinds of arrows. One is tipped with gold that Cupid shoots at someone to cause that individual to fall in love; the other arrow is tipped with lead and when Cupid strikes someone with it, the person repulses a loved one.

In one story, Cupid complains to his mother Venus when a Bee stings him. She laughs and points out that he is small also, and yet delivers the sting as well as bliss of love. Cupid is small, childlike in many ways, rounded in later versions, mischievous, pulling you in by love one minute and in the next, pushing you away. Associated

T

乐

with the element of air, he can also fly like a Bee.

In another myth, Cupid falls in love with Psyche (Soul) but, when she betrays him through weakness, he rejects her and she must pass through many long tests until he forgives and marries her. This is also a quality in Bee hybrids. They are idealistic perfectionists and, if people do not meet their high standards, they could find themselves rejected or abandoned, until a later time when the Bee hybrid might accept that person into their hive again. Simultaneously, Bee hybrids suffer terribly if they are rejected. Being rejected may be a painful, but helpful, challenge in their evolution so they can learn deeper compassion and patience when dealing with others.

I wish to go into some depth showing parallels between Bee and human culture in order to raise our consciousness about Bees, and to see how they and Bee hybrids can be great teachers for us.

There is a wide range of socialness amongst Bee species and also amongst Bee hybrids. They range from solitary ones who do not look after their offspring to honeybees living in communities with 40,000 individuals. This diversity resembles the human world where some individuals, like solitary Bees, only look after themselves as opposed to others …where those we refer to as Queen Bees are in charge of very large organizations.

There are approximately five hundred species of stingless Bees. Like many humans, most are non-violent; whereas some Bees, like humans, prey on others. Cuckoo Bees, for example, lay eggs in the nests of other Bees and their brood eat the larva.

Bees and humans are linked together in a web of life and co-creation. We humans need to look closely at Bees to see the lessons they have for us.

Insects pollinate about one-third of human food and Bees accomplish most of this. Simply put: Without Bees, we don't eat. The bad news is that since 1976, due to colony collapse disorder

(CCD), there has been a dramatic reduction in Honeybees across North America and Europe.

CCD is attributed to a combination of factors including chemical fertilizers, insecticides, viruses that alter Bee DNA, fungus, malnutrition from being fed high-fructose corn syrup, electromagnetic radiation, and a change in Bee-keeping practices, which includes migratory Bee keeping, wherein the Bees are moved from place to place and are kept homeless. These unhealthy practices are not only killing Bees, they also are killing humans. When a colony collapses, adult Bees are absent, having abandoned their food stores and their young.

Symptoms occur prior to final colony collapse: 1) there is an insufficient workforce to look after the developing bees, and that force is made up of young adults, and 2) the Bees do not wish to eat the provided food, which is sugar syrup.

Bees mirror for us what we are doing to our own young and to ourselves. Many humans who cannot handle the stressors of modern life are engaged in their own form of CCD. They eat sugar-laden junk food, like that which we are feeding Bees. This results in physical and emotional malnourishment, often leading to collapse and neglect of their children. With more people disabled, fewer individuals are left to carry on the work of those who cannot. This will lead to our own form of colony collapse. We are seeing this everywhere with the deterioration of our health, as well as in our economic, cultural, religious, and family structures.

And what does a healthy hive look like? Bees and Bee hybrids can teach us! In a healthy hive (organization or family unit), each member pulls his or her weight for the good of the whole. Bees have a group soul and, within the group soul, each individual has a specific purpose. Bee hybrids love unconditionally from their heart, although they are not very interested in sex. Bee hybrids think more of looking after the group than their own life. This may be a woman who does not marry or have children, but dedicates herself to the good of the world. This could also be a Queen Bee ordering her own family, her extended family, and even working in an organization to teach everyone to work for the good of the whole. Bee hybrids specialize in co-creation, which is a principal humans will develop in the next two thousand years of the Aquarian Age.

One Bee alone, looking only after itself, does not benefit others and in the world of Bees, the less developed species are solitary. Bees, like humans, are more advanced when they co-create with others for the good of all. In the world of Bees, there is plenty of honey produced, not only for the members of the hive, but also for humans and animals. Likewise, Bee hybrids, through hard work and a generous heart, create abundance that benefits others.

Bee hybrids are quick-witted, talk and move quickly, are somewhat rounded and often have long marriages. Although they are often intense, they also are loyal and have good senses of humor. They may be found in many different professions ranging from acting to environmental outreach to leading biological research and inventions. All for the good of humanity and the Earth.

Bees hum and vibrate on their soul level and being around Bees and Bee hybrids help people raise their spiritual frequency. Bees carry an electrostatic charge whereby they attract other particles in addition to pollen, which become incorporated into their honey. Bee hybrids attract people to them by using this charge, which is a kind of magnetism.

This does not mean that all individuals move into harmony with them. Some may be jealous of the Bee hybrids ability to draw others to them. Bee hybrids, like Bees, can use their tongue to sting someone if they feel threatened, overwhelmed or challenged. This sting may not be a bad thing. Although some people are allergic to

Bee venom, others (such as those with arthritis) might have blocks and need a push to move on with life.

Bee hybrids are highly sensitive to the frequencies of others and are able to pick up feelings from them. This makes them excellent at both receiving and communicating with others. We see this in the uncanny ability of Bees to direct fellow workers to find the best flowers for honey. They know the more they support others in finding what is best for them, the more it will benefit the entire hive. A Bee hybrid's skin is alive and exudes scents and luminescence and their senses of touch and taste are highly developed. They love to touch, but at the same time, they can be overwhelmed when others touch them. They would like to be hugged and come close, but gentleness is required.

Bee hybrids like to be kept up-to-date about all occurrences surrounding them and find it very distressing if people do not share their feelings, thoughts, and just about everything with them. They like being the one others confess to and they are trusted with other people's stories. In English folklore, Bees had to be kept informed by their keepers when something was happening in the family, such as deaths, births, and marriages. It was considered bad luck not to tell Bees for they might leave the hive, stop producing honey, or die.

Physically, Bee hybrids tend to be round and to love food of all kinds. This could include loving to cook and/or eating good food. The Bee hybrid collects friends and information to share with others. They are interested in healing and in all sorts of spiritual things. One of their greatest challenges is to balance doing with being. They might have a tendency to overwork for the good of the hive. They need to learn to balance work with meditation and spiritual practice and to return to the constant Now, where there is no past, present, or future.

*B*ees are loved by Elementals because honey is one of our favorite foods. They exist in our realm, much as they do in your human one, because they hum on a high frequency and feel perfectly at home with us. Also, unlike humans, we are respectful of Bees and would never take honey without first asking.

The Bee beings who came to Earth from Venus were very intelligent. Their work was to hold up the frequency of the Earth, which they did by resonating at a higher frequency than the human beings evolving here. Some Bee beings decided to stay on Earth and to assist with its evolution by becoming hybrids. As a lasting gift to Earth and humans, they also applied to the Karmic Board to hybridize certain insects with some of their qualities. Those insects became the Bees of today and their gift is golden honey.

➤ Bee Hybrid: SUSAN

"One of my earliest memories was of my dad, his brother and friends working together to create my childhood home. It was exciting to watch the walls going up with timber being sawed and creating lots of sawdust. The sawdust was of particular interest to me as the Bees were always in and around it, hovering and buzzing, building their nests in it. As my dad and uncles were building our house, the bees were building theirs. Their fat, round bodies, bold two-tone yellow and black furry orbs mesmerized me. I cupped them in my hands with the sawdust and they would walk up my arms. The humming of their wings was soothing and comforting to me. I never got stung that whole summer and, to this day, I have never been stung.

"Those two events—the men working together to build a house and the bees building hives—imprinted on me the great amount that can be done by a collective. I grew up working in the building trades, in construction working with a team and understanding the satisfaction of many hands working for one purpose. I have owned many other businesses but, when I do a project with a group, it has to feel like family ... wanting the feeling that we are all working for the same purpose.

"I have always had a round body type, no matter what weight I am, with a temperament that can be lethal if provoked. I suffer dreadfully from rejection and was made invisible many times as a child, having parents distracted by their own pain. Home has always been important to me. Wherever I have lived, I take time and pride in creating that special homey feeling. I am always making sure there are guest rooms for others to come and visit and I love to nourish others with food.

Dyslexia gave me other qualities, including an incredible memory. I was also able to see through people's motives and intentions, always saying that I had a strong 'BS meter'. If I go against my instincts, then the consequences are extreme. I went bankrupt because I went against my instincts.

"As I got older, I sought out healers and spiritual teachers, and travelled to far-off lands to learn about the mysteries of life. I feel I came here to learn patience and forgiveness. Anytime these two qualities show up in my life, I know I am in for Big Lessons."

✎ Bee Hybrid: LYNN

"I am naturally short and round, which has been an ongoing issue. I struggle to find acceptance of myself when I am overweight. I am hypersensitive to many things. Medications and stress affect my stomach badly, and the sun gives me red itchy welts and my lips blister. I have developed a skin disorder that is activated by stress. It doesn't sound very good, but when I am living in the now, and loving myself just as whole-heartedly as I love others, the stress that activates my issues dissipates.

"Initially I was not attracted to sex at all. I enjoyed being close and feeling passion, but the act of sex felt wrong. Now, sex has become much larger than a sexual act, and inclusive of the etheric vibrations that can be energetically merged or communicated.

"I have been emotionally spirited since I was a child. When committed to something, I am passionate and give one hundred percent to its success, which in turn becomes my success. I took on everyone's issues as mine and carried a lot of pain and pressure as I took care of others. Maturity has taught me discernment. I no longer accept the responsibility of fighting issues for others when it is their lesson to learn.

"I have come to understand that I am intelligent in many ways. I am a big picture/global thinker. I look at what is good for the whole. I have a gift of communication and have been able to lead organizations and people. I often feel what others are feeling, whether emotional, physical, or spiritual. There is a connection to people I can describe as a flow of energy. I have the ability to speak on behalf of many perspectives because I can put myself in the position of how decisions will affect others.

"I am a busy person; it is inherent in me. Busy like a Bee. In addition to being busy, I am also a perfectionist; everything needs to be done successfully; failure comes at the price of my ego. I am loyal to a fault, and I expect that people who are close to me should reciprocate with the same degree of loyalty. I have acted as a mother to many, always placing their needs ahead of mine, and encouraging harmony as we work together for the ultimate good of everyone. I find failure and disloyalty to be devastating, turning me to reflect inward at what I did and failed to do.

"I grow spiritually as I mature and take time to be present. When I was pre-occupied with buzzing around being busy, I was unaware of spirituality. I had to give up my work as a leader of a large non-profit company, which I conceived and birthed, in order to grow into being me … a mother, a friend, and facilitator of joy, laughter, and the present. As I do my new work in the world, many people have touched my heart. Stillness has been a gift that helps me grow spiritually.

"My joy, laughter, and love have been my greatest gifts. I use humor and laughter to help people feel good and to release pent-up energy that can cause disease. My sensitivity to the environment and energy has forced me to pay attention to everything. That includes how people, environments, medication, etc. affect me and, in order to recognize this, I had to slow down and be present. My life's work is about pollinating people, but as a hybrid, I should not buzz! I need to stay focused in a personal way. People are my honey!"

HELPFUL HINTS FOR
BEE HYBRIDS

1. You often go on the defensive when there is no need, and feel that others do not appreciate or love you. Relax. Know you are seen and loved by many more than you recognize in your hive.

2. You are naturally round. Round is beautiful.

3. You have a gift to see into people's souls and can tell a truthful person from a con artist. Don't doubt this gift and refuse to be subsumed by the opinions of others.

4. You are here to teach interdependence—and to learn independence. Recognize that loneliness is part of the journey.

5. Forgiveness is essential to your well-being. You can see the truth in others and yourself and still forgive them and yourself.

ANUNNAKI

The next species of hybrid to be discussed is a Star race with many physical and psychological commonalities with humans. They are called the Anunnaki. This term was made popular by Zecharia Sitchin in his book *The 12th Planet*. I do not agree with everything that Sitchin has said about the Anunnaki but there are too many collaborating myths about this race to ignore their presence on our planet.

During the Lemurian cycle approximately 400,000 years ago, extra-planetary beings created a colony on Earth. They were more advanced than the primitive humans on Earth at that time. The creation myths of the Sumerians predate those of the Old Testament of the Bible and are very detailed in their description of these extra-planetary beings. According to the accounts, Anunna prisoners (called Anunnaki by the Babylonians) were sent to Earth because of unacceptable behavior on their own planet. In the Torah, they may be the same ones Ezekiel calls the "fallen ones", the Nephilim, who were said in the Bible to be very large and given to war and interbred with humans.

Anunnaki came in primitive spacecraft, not unlike those NASA builds, and their penance likely involved mining gold in Africa, which archaeological evidence has shown is the location from which the earliest humans have come. (More about this is found in *Decoding Your Destiny*.)

The Anunnaki prisoners were sent here because their own planet couldn't continue its evolution as the frequency of these individuals was holding the others back. Overseers from the same race accompanied these prisoners and kept them from interacting with early humans, the Els, and other advanced races assisting with the evolution of the native inhabitants. Although these Anunnaki were physically, technically, and mentally evolved, they were not very evolved emotionally or spiritually.

Els and Pleiadians were concerned about the prisoners coming to Earth, but they did not stop the event from occurring. They realized that humanity had to develop free will to become conscious creators, and that protecting humanity from other races would not allow this to happen.

The Anunnaki prisoners, not happy with their lives, and for good reason, overthrew their guards. Because they could not return to their home planet, they wanted to make their life more enjoyable on Earth, so they started genetic engineering and mentally imprinting early humans and animals. They made humans cleverer so they could work as slaves in the household and on farms, and sometimes they combined human genes with those of animals. The pig was one of these creations.

Some prisoners, however, had a change of heart and decided to commit to helping the Els and other sentient races according to the Divine Plan. Some of the overseers decided to stay voluntarily to clean up the mess they had been unable to prevent. At present on the Earth, there are Anunnaki hybrids, who were originally both overseers and prisoners. Many of the former prisoners have reformed; others have not.

Anunnaki hybrids may or may not be aware of their original evolution, as is the same with any hybrid. If you discover you are a hybrid of this race and are on a spiritual path practicing love and compassion, dispense immediately with any feeling of guilt or shame of what you may or may not have done in the past. All humans, regardless of their original evolution, have had many setbacks on the path to consciousness. Furthermore, the Anunnaki have not been on Earth for as many lifetimes as most hybrids, so they have not had as much time to adapt to other species here.

Every hybrid race has specific talents and those of this race involve genetic engineering, science, computers, finance, the war industry, and new technologies. Anunnaki hybrids typically have strong will and mental strength and are brilliant at strategic thinking and long-term planning. These hybrids might have a kind of autism, which is a lack of compassion and empathy for others. The weaknesses of these hybrids are arrogance, self-importance, and using their will and logical reasoning to dominate others. The mind of these hybrids is strong enough to hypnotize or mentally imprint others—a quality known to magicians and practiced by many unreformed Anunnaki.

Not all Anunnaki were prisoners on Earth. Many were caretakers concerned with protecting the Earth from the havoc that unreformed Anunnaki might create. They may be fully functioning in society and, as with all hybrids, engaged in various kinds of work.

Unreformed Anunnaki hybrids still want to keep humanity enslaved to their wishes. They are currently concerned about humanity waking up. These hybrids seek to control technologies—media, television, Internet—and food and power systems to keep humans under their control. The good news is they cannot progress to the next phase of human evolution unless they surrender to Divine Will. It is difficult for Anunnaki hybrids to do this, as they are driven by ego and their ego has often provided them with a great deal of material success.

Surrendering personal will to Divine Will is a spiritual law and a necessary step that applies to all beings in their journey to consciousness.

Anunnaki come from a martial culture where only the strong

survive; where others are regarded as threats or victims to be manipulated. They look for any opportunity to defeat an opponent. As such, they are brilliant strategists who can see five steps beyond what most people see. Unreformed Anunnaki hybrids will pretend to be generous and compromising as another strategy to gain control over others. They see gentle, forgiving qualities as weaknesses they can use to get their own way. Even reformed hybrids respect people who challenge them mentally, who have strong will power or resonate at a high spiritual frequency, which they interpret as having power.

Never forget: Anyone can decide to change, and this includes former prisoners. Any of us can use our gifts in ethical or non-ethical ways and many Anunnaki (both the caretakers and reformed) invent technologies that create long-term health and sustainability for humanity. They also work undetected in industries in which they excel to impede the success of unreformed Anunnaki. A rule of thumb is that the longer a reformed Anunnaki hybrid has been dedicated to serve the Divine and not their own will, the greater their empathy, compassion, and desire to be of service to others. Because they have such strong wills, they make great progress in these qualities after they have committed to do so.

Respect is very important to Anunnaki hybrids, and they blossom when they are in environments where their gifts are appreciated. They are natural entrepreneurs, each one a law unto him or herself, and they have difficulties working for others unless they have a great deal of independence. That said, as Anunnaki hybrids evolve, knowing their own weakness, they often seek opportunities to live or work with loving, compassionate individuals in order to develop their weak areas.

The Anunnaki initially set humanity back and caused them to fall off the path of Divine Will that was introduced by the Els,

Angels, and other Star races. They did this by teaching humans to be like them—selfish and self-serving—which closed humans off to the Star Beings resonating in higher frequencies who were guiding them.

However, the Anunnaki have actually benefited humanity in the long term because they strengthened our free will. And, if dedicated to serve Divine Will, that is the quality most essential to becoming a full creator.

*E*lementals have had our own difficulties with the Anunnaki in the past. Because they are so much stronger in will and mental powers, we were no match for them, especially in our early years, and they used their thoughts to change some Elemental evolutions. The unreformed Anunnaki did this for amusement. They created Goblins from Gnomes, which is one reason Goblins are distrustful of humans. Goblins do not differentiate between Anunnaki hybrids and humans because they look alike, and Goblins can see who an individual really is because they had to learn this for self-preservation.

The Anunnaki have strengthened our commitment to learn and develop our free will so we can be co-creators on Earth and protect her. They have also helped us to strengthen our mental body to reason, strategize, and see the larger picture. These were not natural gifts of Elementals, so we have Anunnaki hybrids to thank for this. AND, I would like to add, humans have Anunnaki hybrids to thank for helping them develop these qualities, too.

Hybrids who were overseers may feel deep guilt about failing in their commission to isolate the prisoners from other Earth inhabitants and the problems that have resulted because of this. Reformed Anunnaki hybrids may feel shame for what they have done in the past and feel they need to be punished. These two feelings of shame and guilt may affect their entire lives, although it may be unconscious and they do not know or understand the root cause.

I know several people who have qualities of Anunnaki hybrids. One friend recounted to me a recurring vision. When I mentioned to him about Anunnaki hybrids, he identified with them immediately and said he thought his recurrent vision was true.

⤳ Anunnaki Hybrid: MAURICE

"In the vision I see myself in a spacecraft in the middle of a war in space. I am dressed all in black, a very military-looking uniform, and am working at a console, operating technical flying and fighting equipment that I do not recognize in my present life. I am much taller and broader than present day humans, but I look basically human.

"My side lost the war and we became prisoners. I am sent to a labor camp on Earth and I have to remain there forever and will not be allowed to return to my home planet. The other prisoners who fought alongside me plan to escape and I am torn between going with them or informing the overseers. My dilemma is I am touched by the beauty of the Earth and do not want to harm it. I decide to inform the overseers, even though I risk my life by doing so. The rebellion happened anyway and I was caught. But the overseers believed in my positive intention and sent me to Mesopotamia to work with the Els, who were guardians of Earth.

"Since then, I have sought to ally myself with individuals who are trying to raise the consciousness of humans and the Earth. In this present life, I am very good with computers, larger than most people, and yet cannot handle much stress. I find it extremely difficult to work in a nine-to-five environment. I study various healing techniques, especially those using advanced technologies."

Another friend, Derek, is an atheist and the concept of hybrid star races would be unacceptable to him. However, that does not change the fact that many of the issues and choices he faces in his life are typical of Anunnaki hybrids.

He is a brilliant doctor, well-respected in his field, who has published a great number of papers on new medical treatments. Yet he has made a complete botch of intimate relationships. Derek has been married several times to non-functional or deliberately abusive, coercive women. He seems to believe he deserves this kind of punishment. Derek pushes himself to the limit in anything he does, whether it is physical fitness, work, or hobbies. He must be the best; one of the determining qualities of Anunnaki hybrids.

Both Maurice and Derek appear to have an underlying guilt and shame that shackle them emotionally. Although they are both good people attempting to do good for others, they feel undeserving themselves. I think Derek would have difficulty acknowledging this, although his life choices in intimate relationships testify to it. He has no difficulty attesting to his smartness intellectually and can be smug about others' ability to keep up with him mentally. Anunnaki hybrids typically cannot confess weakness or bad choices.

Both men attempt to be patient with those who are not as fast thinking or able to make in-depth mental leaps from one idea to another. They are both committed to develop more love, patience, tolerance, and forgiveness in their relationships—which is admirable and exactly what an Anunnaki hybrid should learn. They need to apply these same qualities to themselves; to be gentle and know that many people love and respect them as they are.

HELPFUL HINTS FOR ANUNNAKI HYBRIDS

1. Release any guilt or shame about what you might have done to others and the Earth in the past. Use that energy to commit to helping now.

2. Be patient with yourself as you develop love and compassion. Your desire to do so naturally moves you towards opportunities to practice these qualities.

3. Spiritual practice and meditation increase your frequency and will help you move to higher realms to support your wish to serve the Divine Plan.

4. Be on your guard against temptation to serve egoistic goals.

5. Appreciate and honor your strengths that are teaching the rest of us.

OTHER HYBRID POSSIBILITIES

There are other possible hybrids and clues to these are found in many of our myths. These could be descendants of a Lion goddess, such as Sekhmet, the lion-headed goddess with a human body found in the old kingdom of Egypt. Various versions are found in Mesopotamia and in the pre-Vedic civilization of ancient India.

Other legendary beings could also be hybrid composites. For example, the image of the Gryphon is found prior to 2000 BCE in Sumeria. The Gryphon has the body of a lion and the head and wings of a large eagle or hawk-like bird. It could be a hybrid combination of two races, Horus and Sekhmet, possibly created by the Anunnaki, much as they created pigs from mixing humans and animals. Perhaps there is also a Unicorn hybrid, maybe even a Cow hybrid, like Hathor, the Egyptian goddess.

These questions are certainly intriguing, but for now, I am satisfied to have introduced the topic of hybrids and described the most common ones currently evolving on Earth.

Often I am asked if an individual could be one hundred percent human and have no other heredity. At the moment of writing, I think that is doubtful. What is very possible is that an individual has a human origin with another race from the Stars grafted on the original human rootstock. The Star races did this in accordance with the Divine Plan in creating beings on this Earth. Later, the Anunnaki became involved in genetic engineering as well.

CONCLUSION:
HOPE FOR THE FUTURE

*T*he time has come for me last words. This book is something us
Elementals have wanted written for a long time. In our world,
*as you know by now, the various kinds of hybrids described are part
of our everyday existence. They are neighbors, teachers, and fellow
inhabitants of our world. No separation. This world is the etheric-
astral world.*

*Up until now, few humans—beyond the enlightened ones or
close to it—have been conscious in our world ... a higher frequency
than the physical world most humans call Reality. The job of the
Elementals in my group is to create a bridge between you humans
and our world. We do this by telling you more about our world,
because as you open to new possibilities, you let go of your old "it's
only real if you see it" paradigm and extend thought tendrils into
the astral world which anchor here.*

*With this anchor, we can send you new ideas in dreams, visions,
meditations, and "ah ha's"—and guide you to books and teachers to
help you develop consciousness in the astral world.*

*All is going well as the bridge between our worlds has become
increasingly solid, thereby allowing more people to travel across.
Over the next few thousand years, humans will become conscious
in our world and freely befriend and work with the various types of
beings who live in this astral dimension. This includes all species
of Elementals, as well as Angels, Dragons, Inner Earthlings and
others. As humans THINK about hybrids in their physical reality, it
quickens the transition time for our dimensions to meet consciously.*

And now, gentleman that I am, I pass on the VERY last word to Tanis. It has been a pure pleasure and I hope our readers have enjoyed our journey together.

My journey of discovery about hybrids continues. I hope that you are inspired to begin your own exploration, as I feel intuitively that many answers to the perennial questions facing us are answered in travelling along this path of inquiry.

There are many benefits to discovering you are a hybrid, or that people you know may be hybrids. Many hybrids have told me they have a deep sense of rightness about the idea of hybrids in general and more specifically about recognizing the type of hybrid they are when they read the chapter that pertains to them. Many hybrids relate that uncovering this knowledge has called them to deep personal transformation and led them to toss away old cultural and societal norms in which they had forced themselves to fit.

Hybrids often speak about becoming more authentically themselves and how they learned to accept and love themselves more as a result of their discovery. They feel energized and more powerful in their newfound authenticity. One woman even wrote her autobiography after finding out that she was a hybrid. Being comfortable with our hybrid nature is important because, until we are willing to stand naked as our true selves, we waste a great deal of precious life energy hiding behind masks. We do this to keep ourselves safe—safe from letting others fully see us and safe from even seeing ourselves. Both reasons are caused by fear. Our energy, when freed from fear, allows us to fully manifest our Soul's purpose.

The information on hybrids can be of immense service in helping you understand your spouse, children, parents, friends, and work colleagues who you might recognize as being one of these types of hybrids. You will learn how best to deal each person in your life, according to their nature.

Hybrids also share how they now understand why they have difficulties with some types of people more than others, and that the kind of hybrid they are is a polar opposite of the person with whom they have difficulty.

If you discover that you are one of these types of hybrids, you will hopefully find a deeper understanding about WHY you are like you are, as well as more clarity about your life purpose and the gifts you have to achieve your purpose. You will also learn about your weaknesses and be able to develop greater acceptance of yourself, warts and all. It is an immense waste of energy to have guilt and shame about something you may have done in the past. The time to act differently is in the present, now that you have new information and strategies to better handle difficult situations.

Beyond discovering the benefits of being a hybrid to us as individuals, there is a more far-reaching benefit to all humanity and to our planet. If Cosmic Intelligence has allowed so many races of beings to incarnate on Earth, and to create hybrids with humans, there must be a purpose. One or two conscious races (other than human) evolving on this planet might have been accidental, but twenty-two or more sentient races indicate a deliberate Divine Plan.

To me, the reason behind this occurrence is obvious. ALL these races are needed to create life on Earth or Cosmic Intelligence would not have given permission for this to happen. This means all hybrids are necessary to fulfil the collective human destiny of being guardians of Earth. And as we become aware of the great variety of gifts that each hybrid type brings, we can work together to create a healthy, beautiful planet to be enjoyed by all life here.

I believe that Earth is a nursery for Creator gods and that all hybrids need to learn from each other to become full Creators. A human race made up of a myriad of rainbow hues is being created year by year on this planet, and you and I are a part of magnificent growth.

Just look around. In the last few decades, we see the multi-racial, cultural, and religious hybridization that humans are engaged in as white and black people; Asians and Americans, Catholics and Jews intermarry and interbreed. This hybridization of humans is part of the Divine Plan (else it would not be happening), and within a few centuries, as globalization continues, we will find it difficult to find people who are pure anything. Maybe we'll all be the color of golden honey. How wonderful!

We are at the beginning of a new era in human consciousness and each of us is a participant in this grand Cosmic Design. Daily we learn new scientific, biological, psychological, and spiritual facts about our Conscious Universe and our place in it. We are ALL needed to fulfill the Plan.

QUESTIONNAIRE:
WHAT TYPE OF HYBRID AM I?

This quiz will assist you in recognizing the "possible" hybrid you are. It is meant as a **first step** in your personal investigation.

For more detailed analysis, you will find many of the answers you seek in reading about the **twenty-two** different types of hybrids described in this book. You may immediately recognize traits in yourself as you read the various descriptions and, most particularly, the Helpful Hints at the end of each type.

Circle the number of the questions that ring most true for you.

1. Do you have a tendency towards addictions, i.e., drugs, alcohol, sex?

2. Have you been interested in stories about fairies and elves from an early age?

3. Do you sometimes wish you could go to a magical land of beauty and fantasy?

4. Do you have artistic gifts in music, painting, dance, craft, etc.?

5. Would you describe yourself as amoral, androgynous, or sexually ambiguous?

6. Are you highly sensitive to others' vibrations?

7. Are your senses of sight and hearing overly acute or sensitive?

8. Are your interests often ahead of mainstream culture in areas such as light, alternative energy sources, workings of the brain, and/or higher states of consciousness?

9. Would you describe yourself as an introvert and do you have a strong need for aloneness?

10. Do you often relate better to animals or books, than to humans?

11. Do you need to be touched to be healthy, such as through massages and hugs?

12. Do you feel a deep kinship with water beings, such as dolphins and whales?

13. Is it important that you live near water and swim or bathe in it often?

14. Are you working in a healing profession, either physically or emotionally?

15. Does disharmony in your environment deeply upset you?

16. Do you feel strongly that you come from another solar system?

17. Is your relationship with Spirit primary in your life, even ahead of marriage and children?

18. Do you feel you know better than others what is good for them?

19. Do you feel that you are here to serve others, rather than to serve your personal goals?

20. Do you find it difficult waiting for others to catch up to what you know to be true?

21. Do you think quicker than others?

22. Do you have a strong mental capacity to conceptualize and strategize quicker and more thoroughly than other people?

23. Are you impatient with people's ability to keep up with you mentally?

24. Do you find it difficult working with others unless you are the boss or do you prefer to work on your own?

25. Do you have difficulty surrendering your will to either a higher power (God) or to authority figures unless they have proven they deserve your respect?

26. Do you have difficulty saying "No".

27. Would you rather help individuals than a group?

28. Are you drawn to serve those in difficulty, weaker or suffering?

29. Do you have perfect standards for yourself and are hard on yourself when you fall short?

30. Do you think of yourself as a defender of those who cannot defend themselves?

Scoring:

The number of questions you circled "Yes" may direct you to the general category of hybrid you are. Count the "Yes" numbers in each group of FIVE questions, starting with the first five.

If most of your "Yes" answers were in Questions:

- 1 to 5 — you are most likely an Elemental hybrid.
- 6 to 10 — you are more likely a human cousin and have an ancestry from the Inner Earth or Giant.
- 11 to 15 — you are more likely a human cousin and have an ancestry from the Mer, Selkie, Dolphin or Whale heritage.
- 16 to 20 — you may have come from another Star system.
- 21 to 25 — you could be an Anunnaki hybrid.
- 26 to 30 — you are most likely an Angel hybrid.

If you have equal numbers of "Yes" scores in more than one category, there can be several reasons. It can mean that you have lived as more than one type of hybrid on Earth. It may also come from trying to be all things to all people, and either not really knowing or honoring your real self. It may also stem from you choosing the "nice" answers rather than what you consider to be "not as nice" answers. Lastly, you may be an old soul who has lived many incarnations and worn many personalities so many traits are comfortable for you.

For more detailed descriptions of each type of hybrid, please read the description of each one, as well as the Helpful Hints at the end of each description.

ACKNOWLEDGMENTS

I am grateful to the many individuals who have attended my Hybrid workshops and who have encouraged me to write a book about hybrids. It has been a joy doing so and, although I am listed as author (as well as Lloyd the Leprechaun, of course), I thank the many people who have so generously and courageously shared their personal stories of being a hybrid. Although their names are anonymous, many who are close to them will recognize them from their honest and revealing testimonies and I salute their willingness to reveal themselves. Some hybrids have written very detailed stories to me and I am only sorry that, in attempting to include stories from a variety of individuals, I have needed to shorten their accounts.

I wish to thank many people who have helped in various ways. These include, but are not limited to, Basia Alexander, Jonathan Beals, Gudrun Boziat, Oskar Broziat, Darwyn Boucher, Werner Braun, Terry Brown, Sally Burnley, Patty Callaghan, Alice Charland, Jeanne Crane, Ruth Dees, Merle Dulmadge, Gail Elizabeth England, Shelly Ferec-Legall, Darlene Fletcher, Rod Friend, Ann Harley, Laura Harris, Melinda Ewell, Petra Huber, Jenny Lou Linley, Bob Lyons, Ruth McLulich, Katharina Megnet, Bill Menzo, Margaret Mills, Donna Miniely, Willa Miniely, Connie Phenix, Courtenay Pollack, Elyse Pomeranz, Nanson Serriane, Wanja Twan, Marilyn Ward, Christoph Wasser, Derek Whelan.

I am especially grateful to my partner Simon Goede for his thorough listening as I repeatedly read *Hybrids* aloud to him; and to Monika Bernegg, my German translator and friend, who transcribed the recordings from my workshops to provide a base to start the book. In addition, her eagle-eye found errors I missed in the manuscript. Also, I express gratitude to Nita Alvarez who did the professional edit and found yikes many inconsistencies and to my assistant Melany Hallam for a lovely layout and final cover.

Lastly, I would like to thank my agent and friend, the late Bob Silverstein, who believed in my work and encouraged me to write this book. I know he'd like it.

RELATED READING

General Reading on All Hybrids

Tanis Helliwell, *Decoding Your Destiny: Keys to Humanity's Spiritual Transformation*, Wayshower Enterprises, Vancouver, 2012

Many books on myths and religions of various cultures and astronomy have been used during my research but, as always, I rely strongly on inner vision. As this topic has been present in my mind for many years I cannot remember all the television and radio programs, or web references that might have informed my thinking. I offer this list of books about the various hybrids as a starting place. They are categorized alphabetically according to hybrid.

Angel

William Bloom, *Devas, Fairies and Angels: A Modern Approach*, Gothic Image Pub., Glastonbury, 1986

Sophie Burnham, *A Book of Angels*, Galantine Books, New York, 1990

Geoffrey Hodgson, *Kingdom of the Gods*, Theosophical Publishing House, Wheaton

Doreen Virtue, *Messages from your Angels* and many other Angel books, Hay House, California

Peter Lambourne Wilson, *Angels*, Pantheon Books, New York, 1980

Anunnaki

Gerald Clark, *The Anunnaki of Niburu: Mankind's Forgotten Creators, Enslavers, Saviors, and Hidden Architects of the New World Order,*

Createspace, 2013

Zecharia Sitchin, *The 12th Planet*, Avon Books, New York, 1978

Michael Tellinger, *Slave Species of the Gods: The Secret History of the Anunnaki and their Mission on Earth*, Bear and Company, 2012

Centaur

http://www.thecentaurway.com

John Updike, *The Centaur*, Random House, 1996

Dolphin and Whale

Ken Grimwood, *Into the Deep*, William Morrow & Co., New York, 1995

Alexander Jablokov, *A Deeper Sea*, Avon Books, New York, 1992

Sy Montgomery, *Journey of the Pink Dolphins: An Amazon Quest*, Chelsea Green Pub., 2009

Scott Taylor, *Souls of the Sea: Dolphins, Whales, and Human Destiny*, Frog Books, 2003

Dragon

R. A. MacAvoy, *Tea with the Black Dragon*, Bantam Books, New York, 1983

Old Forge, *Dragons*, 1998

(There are many wonderful children's books about Dragons, but those for adults are sorely missing.)

Elemental

Nancy Arrowsmith, *A Field Guide to the Little People*, Pan Books, London, 1977

Lady Gregory, *Visions and Beliefs in the West of Ireland*, Gerrards Cross, Smythe, 1970

Tanis Helliwell, *Summer with the Leprechauns: The authorized edition*,

Wayshower Enterprises, Vancouver,1997, 2011

Tanis Helliwell, *Pilgrimage with the Leprechauns*, Wayshower Enterprises, 2010

Dorothy MacLean, *To Hear the Angels Sing*, Lorian Press, 1980

Diarmuid MacManus, *Irish Earth Folk*, The Devin-Adair Company, New York, 1959

Hugh McGowan, *Leprechauns, Legends and Irish Tales*, Victor Gollancz Ltd., London, 1988

Marco Pogacnik, *Nature Spirits & Elemental Beings*, Findhorn Press, Forres, Scotland, 1977

Carol Rose, *Spirits, Leprechauns, and Goblins, An Encyclopaedia*, W.W. Norton, 1996

Machelle Small Wright, *Behaving as if the God in all Life Mattered*, Perelandra, Warrenton, VA, 1987

Dora Van Gelder, *The Real World of Fairies*, Quest Books, Wheaton, Ill. 1994

W. B. Yeats, *Irish Fairy and Folk Tales*, Modern Library, New York, 1893

El

Kings James version of *The Bible*, Collins, New York, 1953

N.K. Sanders, *Poems of Heaven and Hell from Ancient Mesopotamia*, Penguin, London, 1971

Robert Temple, *The Sirius Mystery*, Destiny Books, Rochester, 1998

Horus

J. J. Hurtak, *The Book of Knowledge: The Keys of Enoch*, 1982

Elisabeth Haich, *Initiation*, Aurora Pub. 2000

Inner Earth Being

John Uri Lloyd, *Etidorhpa*, Pocket Books, New York, 1978.

Mariana Stjerna, *Agartha—The Earth's Inner World*, Soullink, Pub. 2013

Merperson
Kit Whitfield, *In Great Waters*, Ballantine Books, New York, 2009
Skye Alexander, *Mermaids: The Myths, Legends, and Lore*, Adams
    Media, New York, 2012

Pan
Michael Roads, *Talking with Nature and Journey into Nature*, H. J.
    Kramer, 2003.
Michael Roads, *Through the Eyes of Love, Journeying with Pan (Book
    one)*, Six Degrees Pub. Group, 2013

Selkie
David Thomson, *The People of the Sea*, Counterpoint, 2000

ABOUT THE AUTHOR

Tanis Helliwell, M.Ed. is the founder of the International Institute for Transformation. Since January, 2000, IIT has offered programs to assist individuals in becoming conscious creators to work with the spiritual laws that govern our world. Tanis, a mystic in the modern world, has brought spiritual consciousness into the mainstream for over thirty years.

She is the author of *Summer with the Leprechauns, Pilgrimage with the Leprechauns, Decoding Your Destiny, Manifest Your Soul's Purpose, Embraced by Love* and *Take Your Soul to Work.* Her DVDs, *Elementals and Nature Spirits* and *Spiritual Transformation: Journey of Co-creation,* as well as her Personal Growth and Inner Mysteries CDs are helpful to individuals who want to work with Elementals and other sentient beings evolving on Earth.

She is a student and teacher of the Inner Mysteries, living on the seacoast north of Vancouver, Canada. Since childhood, she has seen and heard Elementals, Angels, and master teachers in higher dimensions. Tanis conducted a psychotherapy practice for thirty years, helping individuals with their spiritual transformation. To heal the Earth and catalyze individual transformation, she led tours and walking pilgrimages to sacred sites around the world for over twenty years.

Tanis Helliwell is a sought-after keynote speaker whose insightful awareness is applied in a variety of spiritual disciplines. She has presented at conferences featuring Rupert Sheldrake, Matthew Fox, Barbara Marx Hubbard, Gregg Braden, Fritjof Capra, and Jean Houston. These conferences include The Science and Consciousness Conference in Albuquerque, The World Future Society in Washington, D.C., and Spirit and Business conferences in Boston, Toronto, Vancouver, and Mexico City. Tanis has also presented at Findhorn, Hollyhock, A.R.E. Edgar Cayce and Alice Bailey conferences.

Tanis works a great deal in Europe and with psychiatrists, medical practitioners, and other healers to clear the etheric and astral bodies in developing healthy consciousness.

To write to the author, order books, CDs and DVDs, or for information on upcoming workshops, please contact:

Tanis Helliwell
1766 Hollingsworth Rd.,
Powell River, BC., Canada V8A 0M4
E-mail: tanis@tanishelliwell.com

WEB SITES:

www.tanishelliwell.com
www.iitransform.com
www.facebook.com/Tanis.Helliwell

BOOKS:

- Summer with the Leprechauns: the authorized edition
- Pilgrimage with the Leprechauns: a true story of a mystical tour of Ireland
- Decoding Your Destiny: keys to humanity's spiritual transformation
- Manifest Your Soul's Purpose
- Take Your Soul to Work
- Embraced by Love

DVDs

1. Elementals and Nature Spirits
2. Spiritual Transformation: Journey of Co-creation
3. Take Your Soul to Work
4. Managing the Stress of Change

CDs

Series A — Personal Growth Collection: Two Visualizations

1. Path of Your Life / Your Favorite Place
2. Eliminating Negativity / Purpose of Your Life
3. Linking Up World Servers / Healing the Earth

Series B — Inner Mysteries Collection: Talk and Visualization

1. Reawakening Ancestral Memory / Between the Worlds
2. The Celtic Mysteries / Quest for the Holy Grail
3. The Egyptian Mysteries / Initiation in the Pyramid of Giza
4. The Greek Mysteries / Your Male and Female Archetypes
5. The Christian Mysteries / Jesus' Life: A Story of Initiation
6. Address from The Earth / Manifesting Peace on Earth

Series C –

1. The Body Elemental / Healing with the Body Elemental
2. Rise of the Unconscious / Encountering Your Shadow